Birds of Eastern China

Brian Westland

Arctic Warbler (Pylloscopus borealis)

(12 cm.) Larger than other warblers; long yellow stripe over eye; bill slightly upturned; single wing bar.

Most of the birds described in these pages are found in China throughout the year. For most of us in Eastern China, the only chance we will get to see this bird is during its lengthy spring and fall migrations along China's East Coast. During the months of April and May in spring and August and September in fall, there is a very good chance to see this bird darting through the trees of city parks and gardens.

The Arctic warbler undertakes one of the longest migrations of any Asian or European songbird. During the summertime breeding season, this species can only be found in the extreme north of China, in northern Heilongjiang province. Most members of the species breed in Russia in a region approaching the Arctic Circle. This liking for extreme northern latitudes gives the bird its name.

The Arctic Warbler is a member of a large family of warblers, "Acrocephalinae." China is home to no less than 83 species of warblers. All warblers are small, extremely active insectivores that consume no other food besides insects. The limited nature of their diet dictates that these birds must always be in a place where insects are found, thus all warbler species that breed in locations which get too cold to support insect life in winter must fly south to warmer climates. The Arctic Warbler flies as far south as Indonesia and the Philippines to sustain itself in winter.

The Arctic Warbler is part of a subgroup of warblers known as "leaf warblers." This group includes all the Asian warblers that are usually seen foraging high in trees for insects. Other species of warblers may choose to hunt on the ground for food or perch along rivers or ponds. All leaf warblers have greenish backs and white under parts with similar markings making identification very difficult. This species can usually be distinguished by its single wing bar, larger size and slightly upturned bill.

During spring and fall migrations, several species of leaf warblers can often be seen together foraging for food among the treetops. Leaf warblers move quickly while feeding leaping from branch to branch in a state of perpetual motion. Under these conditions it is often impossible to identify which species one is observing. Even seasoned birdwatchers are hard pressed to make sure species identifications on most days.

Arctic Warbler (Photo by Charles Lam)

Asian Brown Flycatcher (Muscicapa dauurica)
(13 cm.) Small; grey-brown upperparts; whitish underparts; eye-ring

The Asian Brown Flycatcher is a rather nondescript species of the flycatcher family, but it is so seemingly ubiquitous throughout much of its range that it deserves to be acknowledged in any description of birds in China. As with other flycatchers, this species is usually spotted while it sits motionless on an exposed perch waiting for passing flying insects on which to pounce.
It is a uniformly grey-brown bird with whitish under parts without striking markings. It does possess a thin white eye ring which is only sometimes noticeable.

There are several other nondescript grey-brown flycatchers in Eastern China, but they are nowhere as common as this species. The Grey-streaked Flycatcher has a similar appearance to this species, but also has conspicuous streaks on its under parts.

The Asian Brown Flycatcher breeds in Northeast China and migrates along the country's East Coast to wintering grounds in southeast China, including the island of Hainan and as far south as Indonesia.

This species favors open woodlands and cultivated areas where trees are well spread out. The bird nests in tree cavities, perhaps in an abandoned woodpecker nest. The female bird will typically lay four eggs which will be incubated by the female exclusively.

When hunting for food, the Asian Brown Flycatcher displays the peculiar habit of flicking its tail when returning to its perch following its attempts.

Asian Brown Flycatcher (Photo by K Hari Khrisnan)

Azure winged Magpie (Cyanopica cyanus)
Field marks: (31-35 cm.) Black head, blue wings, long blue tail, and white underparts

The Azure-winged Magpie is a close cousin of the "lucky bird" of China, the Black-billed Magpie. It is easy to recognize the physical similarities between the two species as both share a long slender body, long tail and long bill, but these two species, while sharing a family heritage seem to differ in personality.

The Black-billed Magpie is a noisy and aggressive bird that is often seen attacking and harrying other species. The Azure-winged Magpie, on the other hand is a relatively shy and docile bird that is difficult to approach. In large cities, such as Beijing, these birds have become much tamer due to their exposure to friendly humans in city parks.

Like its more boisterous cousin, the Azure-winged Magpie is an omnivore that sustains itself by eating a wide variety of foods. It will eat insects as well as pine seeds and acorns, the large seeds of the oak tree. Given its more diffident temperament, the Azure-winged Magpie is less likely to engage in predatory behavior, and as such, it has not earned the negative reputation of its bigger cousin.

This species can readily be found in city parks as these locations offer both the coniferous and deciduous trees that provide it with food and shelter. Outside of the city, the Azure-winged Magpie can be found in coniferous or deciduous forests.

The Azure-winged Magpie is a gregarious bird that likes the company of others of its kind. It is usually found in large loose flocks, especially in fall at the end of the breeding season. Following the completion of breeding and chick-rearing duties, magpies will band together to search for food. Flocks of 50-60 individuals can be seen gleaning the treetops of forests and moving together from tree to tree.

The Azure-winged Magpie will also nest in colonies with each pair of mated magpies having its own tree in which to make a nest. The female magpie usually produces around 6-8 eggs and incubate them for about two weeks before hatching.

Azure-winged Magpie (Photo by Toshiro Gamo)

Barn Swallow (Hirunda rustica)
Field marks: (20cm.) forked tail, blue above, white below, rusty throat

The Barn Swallow is a common and cosmopolitan bird that can be found in Europe, Africa, Asia, and all over the Americas. It is the most widespread member of the swallow family. In China, this species can found be found everywhere except certain locations in the West such as Tibet. The males and females of all swallow species look alike.

All swallows are included in the large "songbird" group, generally considered to be those birds that are placed in the order, "Passeriformes." Their streamlined beauty and acrobatic flights make them engaging birds to observe.

Like flycatchers, all swallows are insectivores that actively hunt their insect prey. Swallows do not sit and wait for insects like flycatchers, however, they dive and swoop to capture insects in midair expending vast amounts of energy in their attempts to capture food. While pursuing their meals swallows display aeronautic skill unmatched in the bird world.

Barn Swallows get their names from their long-standing relationship with man and their preference for nesting sites close to human habitation. Often, Barn Swallows will nest in barns and stables, but find other forms of man made structure to their liking as well. These structures should be near open country such as pasture, meadows and farmland.

In places where man made abodes are available, Barn Swallows will build nests made of mud, grass and feathers under the overhanging roofs of various types of buildings. If man made buildings are not available, this species will find cliffs with overhangs on which to build their nests. The nests form deep cups and attach to the vertical portion of a structure, such as a wall of a building.

The female Barn Swallow will typically lay 5-6 eggs and incubate them herself while her mate will attend to hunting duties to feed her and the chicks when they hatch.

Barn Swallow (Photo by Andreas Eichler)

Black Drongo (Dicrurus macrocercus) Hei juanwei

(30 cm.) Glossy blue-black; very long, deeply-forked tail

The Black Drongo is a strange looking bird which is a member of the bird tribe, "Dicrurini," the drongos. This tribe, which was once considered a family, includes seven species which can be found in China. The Black Drongo is also known as "King Crow," despite bearing no relation of the crow family.

The Black Drongo is one of the most instantly recognizable birds in China due to its uniformly jet-black plumage and deeply-forked tail. No other completely black bird in China possesses such a tail. Another Drongo species, the Crow-billed Drongo, is also uniformly black, but bears only a slight fork in its tail. The distinctive silhouette of the Black Drongo is a fairly common sight on telephone wires on roadsides throughout much of Eastern China.
The range of this species includes all of India and Southeast Asia. In China, it is found in summer throughout most of the eastern and central part of the country. It is a year long resident in Hainan and Taiwan.

Black Drongos are active very early in the morning in the search of their favorite food, insects. They eat many large insects such as grasshoppers, cicadas, wasps, bees, dragonflies, and beetles. They perch and wait for flying insects in the manner of a flycatcher, and actively chase insects on the wing. At other times they will feed on the ground. In addition to insects, this bird will eat reptiles, other birds and even bats.

Both male and female Black Drongos sing in spring to attract a mate and establish territories. A cup-shaped nest made of thin sticks is placed in the fork of a tree, and the female lays typically three eggs. It is an aggressive bird which frequently attacks larger birds such as crows and birds of prey which have the audacity to invade its territory. The ferocious nature of the Black Drongo encourages several other bird species such as orioles, doves, and bulbuls to nest close to the nests of the Black Drongo for the added protection these birds supply.

Black Drongo (Photo by Ravi Vaidyanathan)

Black-billed Magpie (Pica pica)
Field marks: (45-60cm.) Large; iridescent; black and white; long tail. Black part of the bird appears to be a green or blue in the right angle of light.

The Black-billed Magpie is one of the most familiar birds on the East Coast of China. It is widely known as the "lucky bird" by the Chinese and it is associated with good luck and fortune for those who encounter it.

In fact, this species, while extremely handsome, has a far less attractive disposition and reputation. It should be noted that all species of magpie belong to the avian family, "Corvidae," the same family as the crow and the raven. Several members of the family are associated with bad luck and devilment. Magpies, crows, ravens and jays are all members of the family, and all are among the most intelligent of birds. However, this family also has a reputation for savagery.

The Black-billed Magpie is an omnivore and it will consume a large variety of foods. In addition to eating nuts, seeds and berries, it will take small rodents such as mice. This species, along with several other members of its family, is known to predate on the young of other bird species. It will also attack and bully cats, dogs, and other birds that may venture too close to its territory. It is clearly not a lucky bird for those species upon which it preys and wreaks havoc.

The Black-billed Magpie is also found in the western part of North America. It can be found throughout much of Western North America as well as Asia. It seems to be particularly successful on the East Coast in China, especially around Qingdao where it seems as ubiquitous as people.

This species is non-migratory, unlike most other songbirds. It may wander in order to find new food sources, but it does not undertake large scale migrations in spring and fall.

The Black-billed Magpie frequents open country such as fields and pastures that offer scattered trees. The bird's love of this type of environment makes it an ideal city dweller. Cities offer parks and suburban sprawl that simulate its preferred natural habitat. In the cities, this magpie may be a scourge to other forms of urban wildlife, but it will not bother humans beyond attempts to raid garbage bins.

Like many non-migratory species, the Black-billed Magpie breeds early in spring. It builds a large, domed nest of loosely bound twigs and the female lays 6-10 eggs. Young magpies can fly after about one month after hatching and feed themselves in two months.

Black-billed Magpie (Photo by Brian Westland)

Black-faced Bunting (Embiriza spodocephala)
(14 cm.) Male: Grey head, nape and throat; black lores and chin; upperparts brown with black streaks; pale yellow and white underparts. Female/winter males: olive head; yellow eye stripe; yellow patch below ear.

The Black-faced Bunting is another common and often seen species of bunting which breeds in the central and northern portions of the country and wintering in the far southeast. It can be found everywhere in Eastern China at some point during a calendar year.

Most of the buntings in China are members not only of the same family, but also of the same genus, "Embiriza." Their common membership in the second-most specific level of classification reflects their close DNA relationship to each other as well as a common lifestyle. Like the other buntings mentioned in this book, their diets consist of primarily seeds and grains.

The Black-faced Bunting is fond of bushy habitat and can often be found at the edges of forests. During migration, it is a common sight in city parks and gardens, often in the company of other buntings. This species can often be observed flicking its tail in a manner similar to a pipit of a wagtail.

The Black-faced Bunting breeds in the undergrowth of coniferous forests in Northeast China and Russia. Its nest is found near rivers or streams and can be situated on the ground or in a tree. The female lays 4-5 eggs. When the eggs hatch, the female will feed her offspring on insects, giving the young birds much needed protein to boost their growth. During this time she and her mate will also feed on insects. After the breeding season, the birds will feed exclusively on seeds.

Black-faced Bunting (NIMSoffice at en.wikipedia)

Black-headed Gull (Larus ridibundus)
(40 cm.) White and gray; black head; red bill.

The Black-headed Gull is a common species of gull found in the coastal regions of eastern China. Gulls are the large, noisy white birds that frequent the seasides of all cities. They are often fed by people at sea sides and the birds will often take food from the hands of their human benefactors. All gulls are members of the family, "Laridae."

Eighteen species of gull occur in China and most are quite difficult to identify. This is due to great similarities in appearance, especially among immature birds of certain species. This species, however, is easy to identify and very common also, thus its inclusion here. Unlike some other gull species, this bird is rarely found at sea, far from shore.

Another black-headed species, the Saunder's Gull can be found in the same coastal regions. However, Saunder's Gull is smaller and has a much shorter black bill. The bill of the Black-headed Gull is dull red. In winter, the Black-headed Gulls lack the black head, but can be identified by their long red bills and a black spot behind the eye.

As with all gulls, the Black-headed Gull is primarily a fish-eater, although it will also spend a significant amount of time on scavenging, taking human leftovers as a large part of its diet.

Black headed Gulls breed in Northern China and Russia in large colonies found in marshes and islands found in freshwater lakes. Their nests are simple structures found on the ground

In many coastal areas, this is one of the species of gulls that can become quite tame and familiar with local residents who like to offer food. In close contact with people its laughter-like calls can be readily heard. This species Latin name, "Larus ridibundus," means "laughing gull."

Black-headed Gull (Photo by Dr. S. Natarajan)

Black-naped Oriole (Oriolus chinensis)
(26. cm.) Completely yellow, except for the wing tips and tail; black mask; long pinkish bill

The Black-naped Oriole is a strikingly beautiful yellow and black bird which is a member of the avian family, "Oriolidae," the orioles. All orioles are robust birds with long powerful bills which they employ in the consumption of fruits and insects. The Black-naped Oriole is named for the black patch on the back of its head near the nape of its neck. This patch extends upon the face of the bird to form a mask. Males and females of this species look alike.

This species is Asian in its distribution and it is found in many Asian countries including Russia, Korea, China, India, Burma and Thailand. In China, it is a breeding bird that breeds throughout Eastern China all the way up to Heilongjiang province.

Orioles of all species make nests that resemble bags that are situated in the forks of trees and suspended from branches. Orioles are renowned singers among songbirds and are known for their beautiful and melodious whistled songs.

The Black-naped Oriole is a versatile bird which can eat a wide variety of foods and live in a wide variety of habitats. It can be found in forests, parks and cultivated areas as well.

Their diets consist of a wide variety of insect species in addition to fruits. The bird is especially fond of berries. The Black-naped Oriole possesses a predatory streak like the Black-billed Magpie, and it will often take eggs and chicks from the nests of other songbirds.

During the breeding season, the female of the species may build several nests before finally settling on one suitable for use. The unused nests are often occupied by the males during the breeding season. Nests are often built close to the nests of the Black Drongo. The females lay 2-3 eggs and incubate them herself. Once hatched, the chicks are provided with food by both parents.

The Black-naped Oriole's great beauty is a mixed blessing for this bird in China. While beloved by many birdwatchers, this species is often trapped for the caged bird market in the country. Beautiful birds such as this species should clearly be appreciated where they belong-in the wild.

Black-naped Oriole (Photo by JM Garg)

Blue and White Flycatcher (Cyanoptila cyanomelana)

(17 cm.) Male: Face, throat and breast black; upperparts blue; underparts white. Female: Grey-brown upperparts; brown wings and tail; white down center of throat and belly.

The Blue and White Flycatcher's name is a descriptive moniker which goes a long way to explain this bird's appearance and behavior. The male of the species is largely blue and white, but it also has large patches of black on the face and throat. The female, like many songbirds, is a much less beautiful bird than the male.

The bird's family, "flycatcher," or "Muscicapidae" is a group of generally small songbirds which engage in active forms of hunting for flying insects such as flies. Many species of this family found in China are brightly colored. They are often seen sitting motionless on a perch, usually a protruding branch of a tree, waiting for a flying insect to pass before they launch themselves on a short flight to attempt to capture their prey.

The Blue and White Flycatcher if somewhat larger than other flycatchers and its striking coloration makes it one of the most beautiful to behold.

This species, like all members of its family, is highly migratory, and in fact, is only visible in many locations in the country during its migrations. It is fairly common, however, and given a little effort on the part of the observer, it can be found often during migration.

In summer, this bird breeds through Korea and Northern China, it migrates the entire length of the East Coast of China to its wintering grounds in South China, the Philippines, and Malaysia.

The Blue and White Flycatcher shows a preference for wooded areas such as deciduous forests. It can often be seen hunting and feeding high in the forest canopy.

This species is fond of all kinds of insects, not only flying ones. While smaller flycatchers will content themselves with the pursuit of flying insects, this species will often be seen searching the ground for insects and other invertebrates such as millipedes and centipedes.

Blue and White Flycatcher (Photo by Brian Westland)

Bohemian Waxwing (Bombycilla garrulous)
(18 cm.) Silky brown-grey plumage; black mask; head crest; waxy white, yellow and red "droplets" on wings.

The Bohemian Waxwing is a bird of exquisite beauty that is, unfortunately, an uncommon bird in China. Due to their uncommon status, beholding one is all the more exciting. Two species of waxwing can be found in China, this species and the similarly uncommon Japanese Waxwing. Both species are beautiful crested birds with black masks and uniformly brown-grey plumage.

The Bohemian Waxwing is easily distinguished from the Japanese Waxwing by the yellow tip of its tail, and more colorful, wax-like decorations on its wings. All three waxwing species in the world, these two species and the Cedar Waxwing of North America are named for the wax-like adornments on the birds' wings. All have soft silky-looking feathers.

The Bohemian Waxwing is the only waxwing found throughout the Northern Hemisphere. Its name, "Bohemian," means "wanderer," a reference to its wide range. In China, the Bohemian Waxwing is an irregular breeding bird of Heilongjiang's Hinggan Mountains. It will not be found elsewhere in China in the summer. In winter, it is a regular, but not completely reliable visitor to "dongbei" and the Liaoning, Shandong, Hubei, Jiangsu region.

The Bohemian Waxwing has a gentle nature that is befitting of its physical beauty. It is primarily a consumer of berries, and berry shortages in northern latitudes influence its irregular winter wanderings. In addition to berries, the Bohemian Waxwing will eat insects during the breeding season.

The Bohemian Waxwing usually nest high in a pine tree, but it will choose other nesting locations depending on the availability of food supplies. Mated pairs of this species often have more than one nest in a particular area. Usually 4-6 eggs are laid by the female in a nest lined with moss, grass and down. Young Bohemian Waxwings develop quickly and are independent about one month after hatching.

Bohemian Waxwing (Photo by Randen Pederson)

Brambling (Fringilla montifringilla)

(16 cm.) Male: Reddish-brown breast; white rump; white belly; black head and nape Female: Similar to male but with brown head

The Brambling is another widespread bird species that can be found in China and in many places outside of the country. It is a finch, as are sparrows, buntings and grosbeaks, and specifically, it is a member of the subfamily, "Fringillinae." This group of finches differs from others in several basic ways.

These finches generally possess smaller bills than other finches, although their bills are still much thicker than those bills of other songbird species. All species of finch require thick bills to enable their nut and seed eating diets. These birds also make open cup-shaped nests which differ from the domed nests of some other finches. As a group, the members of the Fringillinae family are nervous birds that are difficult to approach. They all possess slightly longer notched tails than other finches as well.

The Brambling is an attractive bird with bold markings. The male of the species has a rusty breast which contrasts with the black of its head, wings and back. It has white "shoulder" patches near the wings. All in all it is a handsome species, indeed. The female displays a similar pattern, but has a grayish head and back.

The Brambling can be found throughout most of eastern China during the winter months. It can be found in all types of forest and well-treed parks and gardens.

The Brambling shares a rather odd habit with another Chinese finch, the Black-faced Bunting. Like the bunting, the Brambling, although a largely seed-eating species, will feed its young insects. This practice makes sense as insects contain the protein which can boost growth in chicks. Other finch species will feed their young seeds, not insects.

The Brambling's nest is placed in the forks of a tree, and it is painstakingly decorated with moss or lichens to help conceal it from predators. The female Brambling deposits 4-8 eggs in her camouflaged nest.

Brambling (Photo by Maartin Visser)

Brown Shrike (Lanius cristatus)
(20 cm.) grayish above; light brown below; black eye "mask"

The Brown Shrike, like all members of the shrike family, is a seeming contradiction in the bird world. While it is a technically a songbird, its lifestyle is better suited to an eagle, hawk, owl or other raptor. Like these birds, it is a predator of other birds and small mammals.

The word, "songbird," is generally used for members of the order, "Passeriformes," and refers to small birds such as sparrows, warblers and thrushes which usually perch in trees, and in breeding season, sing beautiful songs. Songbirds are generally gentle creatures that are frequent victims of predators and not predators themselves. Shrikes are the exceptional in this regard. All shrikes possess slightly hooked bills which only hint at their aggressive mode of operation.

In addition to actively hunting and killing birds and small mammals, all members of the shrike family reserve a supply of food for use during hard times. They do this by impaling dead mice, birds, and large insects on the thorns of certain species of bushes.

The Brown Shrike feeds mainly on large insects such as grasshoppers and butterflies, but it will also hunt and kill small birds and lizards. A Brown Shrike is usually observed sitting atop a perch on an exposed tree branch while watching the ground below. From its perch, the shrike will launch its assault on potential prey items.

Like other largely insectivorous bird species, the Brown Shrike is highly migratory. As insects are not available in northern latitudes during winter, this bird will undertake a lengthy migration from its breeding range in Northern China, Mongolia and Siberia to its wintering grounds in Hainan, the Philippines, and Taiwan. Brown Shrikes usually return to exactly the same wintering grounds each winter.

The Brown Shrike returns to its breeding grounds late in the spring when a large population of insects is available. This usually occurs during late May to early June. The species builds nests in small trees or bushes, and the female bird will typically lay 2-6 eggs.

Brown Shrike (Photo by JM Garg)

Buff-bellied Pipit (Anthus rubescens)
(15 cm.) Small; brown upperparts; heavily streaked underparts; black patch on side of neck.

The Buff-bellied Pipit, also called American Pipit, is a common bird in Central and Southeast China during the winter season. Like the Dusky Thrush, its breeding range is entirely to the north of Mainland China, so it is generally not seen in this country during the summer months of the breeding season.

All pipits are members of the family, "Motacillidae." They are all brown, rather plain-looking birds with fine streaks on their bellies. Pipits are usually found walking on the ground searching for insects among leaves and other scattered debris. If approached too close they will usually fly up to the branch of a nearby tree and wait for the intruder to leave. Once the danger has passed they will fly back down to the ground and resume their foraging.

The Buff-bellied Pipit is a small pipit with extensive streaking on its breast and sides. Males and females look alike.

All species of pipits resemble sparrows with the most familiar sparrow to the locals of Eastern China being the Eurasian Tree Sparrow. However, although sparrows and pipits are all brown birds with generally brown backs and lighter, often white under parts, there are significant differences. Sparrows possess the thick, conical bills required of a seed eater, while pipits have thin bills adapted for picking insects from the underbrush. These birds differ in their gaits, as well. Sparrows hop from place to place while pipits walk around like a bipedal hominid. Pipits also possess the odd habit of wagging their tails almost constantly.

Although the Buff-bellied Pipit is not likely to be seen in China during summer, at other times such as during spring and fall migrations and in winter, it is a common and fascinating bird. It can easily be found in city parks, university campuses and other places that offer open and grassy terrain.

Buff-bellied Pipit (Photo by Alan Vernon)

Bull-headed Shrike (Lanius bucephalus)
(19 cm.) Male; Brown; brown head crown; white-tipped tail; grey back; black mask
Female: Duller; brown ear patch

The Bull-headed Shrike is a common resident of East China just like its cousin, the Brown Shrike. As a member of the shrike family it shares its family's love of predation and habits regarding the storage of prey species (see Brown Shrike for more details).

The Bull-headed Shrike, like all shrikes, has a conspicuous mask on the side of its face. Its plumage is darker than the Brown Shrike. Female shrikes are generally duller versions of the males.

This species lives in a similar range in East China to that of the Brown Shrike, but has a more limited breeding range that is restricted to the provinces of southern

Heilongjiang, Liaoning, Hebei, and as far south as Shandong. In winter, it can be found in much of South China from around Shanghai south along the East Coast to Shenzhen. The wintering grounds of the Brown Shrike are limited to a small area around Hong Kong/Shenzhen.

The Bull-headed Shrike shares the Brown Shrike's fondness for open and cultivated habitat including city parks where it can be found sitting on an exposed perch patiently waiting for passing insects and vertebrates such as lizards. It is also known to consume crustaceans in places where they can be found.
In breeding season, the female of this species will lay 2-6 eggs in a nest nestled in a bush or a bamboo tree. She will incubate them for 2 weeks until hatching. Young shrike chicks will be fully-feathered (fledged) in an additional two weeks.

The voice of this bird is harsh and chattering. Like other shrikes, it will often mimic the calls of other bird species in order to draw them close before killing them.

Bull-headed Shrike (Photo by Brian Westland)

Chinese Pond Heron (Ardeola Bacchus)

(47 cm.) Breeding season: Small heron; white wings; head, neck and breast dark brown; white underparts. In winter: Heavily streaked brown heron; white with brown back in flight.

The Chinese Pond Heron is a member of a large family of mostly freshwater birds, "Ardeidae," that includes many long-legged species such as herons, egrets and bitterns that stalk fish and other aquatic species in rivers, ponds, and lakes. All members of this family are closely related and share similar lifestyles despite bearing various labels such as "herons" or "egrets" or "bitterns."

All these birds are equipped with adaptations that enable them to be successful hunters in their watery habitats such as long necks and long dagger-like bills that are employed to spear fish, frogs, lizards and other species of vertebrate and invertebrate prey.

Herons can easily be confused with other long-legged bird species such as cranes, ibises, and storks, but they do have generally sharper, more knife-like bills, and in flight, herons pull their necks in close to their bodies, while these other birds fly with necks outstretched.

The Chinese Pond Heron, although large, is a medium-sized bird of its family. Some members of the family such as the Grey Heron can approach 100 cm. in length. This species is called a "pond heron" due to its particular fondness for ponds as hunting grounds. In China, it is often found in the rice fields of the south.

The Chinese Pond Heron is a striking bird in the breeding season with a dark brown head and neck contrasting with its white breast and belly and blue back.

This bird will frequent both fresh and salt water ponds and wetlands. This species' diet consists of the fish, insects and crustaceans.

This species, like other herons, is a community nester in the breeding season. It forms loose colonies of nesting birds often including other species of herons. These community nesting places are often called, "heronries." The female Chinese Pond Heron usually lays a clutch of 3-6 blue-green eggs. The breeding range consists of the eastern half of China from approximately Jilin Province in the North to around Fujian Province in the South and extending westwards to Sichuan Province

Chinese Pond Heron (Photo by JJ Harrison)

Collared Scops Owl (Otis lettia)

(24 cm.) Large for a scops owl; ear tufts; pale brown "collar" extending around back of neck; dark brown eyes.

Owls are often viewed with fear and superstition by many cultures in the world, including the Chinese. It is likely the birds' fixed and unblinking gaze, nocturnal habits, and eerie, ghost-like calls that have earned them distrust by much of humankind.

The Collared Scops Owl is a resident species throughout almost all of Eastern China, only missing in western parts of Heilongjiang and Jilin. It is only partially migratory.

This species is found in woodlands and parks where trees are in abundance. It is one species of owl which has managed to become an urban resident in China, It can be found in the Eastern Chinese cities in residential areas where trees are plentiful.

The female Collared Scops owl nests in a tree, like most other owl species. It generally lays 3-5 eggs.

Several other species of Scops owls can be found in China and one other, the Oriental Scops Owl, is found in the east. All Scops owls are small and have "ears," the feathered tufts which look like a cat's ears. All other owl species in China will likely be found far from human habitation, however.

Collared Scops Owl (Photo by Santosh Namby Chandran)

Common Buzzard (Buteo buteo)

(55 cm.) Large; upper parts dark reddish-brown; brown "mustache'," underparts whitish; In flight: wide, rounded wings; white patch near the base of primary feathers; usually has a black bar near tip of tail

The Common Buzzard is a large "bird of prey." It is one of several species of hunting birds with certain adaptations for the killing of other birds, reptiles, and small mammals. Birds of prey are all armed with sharp, powerful claws on their feet called, "talons." It is the talons of these birds that usually perform the killing task. All birds of prey also have sharply hooked bills designed by nature for tearing flesh. Eagles, buzzards, falcons, ospreys, and owls are all considered birds of prey. At times, these birds are also called "raptors."

The Common Buzzard and other raptors which are placed in the genus, "Buteo," are referred to individually as "hawks" in North America, or "buteos" as a group. These birds are usually called "buzzards" in Europe and Asia.

All buzzards are fairly large raptors with broad bodies, wings, and tails. They are usually seen soaring in the skies overhead in a seemingly effortless fashion. All buzzards are masters of this energy-conserving mode of flight that takes advantage of rising columns of heated air called "thermals" by birders. In summer, these thermals can enable buzzards and other birds of prey to soar for several hours without any movement of their wings.

Although a variety of names are given to raptors in different parts of the world, their scientific names are standardized world-wide. The Common Buzzard, along with other buzzards, eagles and vultures are all part of the family, "Accipitrinae."

The Common Buzzard, as its name suggests, is a common member of its family, and indeed it is a common sight in the skies along the East Coast of China during its spring and fall migrations. It is large buzzard that can be identified from below by its very broad and rounded wings. Other eastern buzzards have thinner and more square-shaped wings. This bird is a master of soaring and it is often seen to hover in one spot.

This species breeds in coniferous forests in the northeast provinces of the country and winters in the south central part of China from around Shanghai in the north down to Hainan, Hong Kong and Taiwan.

Common Buzzard (Photo by Dick Daniels)

Common Crane (Grus grus)
(105 cm.) Large; grey; crown is black and red; neck grey; white stripe down back of neck

The Common Crane is a member of the crane family, "Gruidae." All cranes are very large birds with long legs and long bills which are designed for wading and feeding in grassy and aquatic habitats. Although they bear a close resemblance to herons and egrets, cranes are not closely related to these birds. In China, cranes have long been symbols of longevity. This species is also known as the Eurasian

Crane. Despite its name, the Common Crane is declining in numbers and might be described as "increasingly uncommon."

The Common Crane is found throughout most of Northern Europe and Asia in the summer. It undertakes long migrations from its summer breeding grounds to locations far to the south such as Africa, South Europe and South Asia. In China, this species breeds in the extreme northeast portion of the country and winters in the southern half of the eastern portion.

During its long migrations, flocks of this species can be seen flying in unison in a "V" formation. When seen in flight, cranes can be distinguished from herons by their outstretched necks. Herons fly with their necks tucked in close to their bodies. During their migrations Common Cranes will often stop to rest and feed in cultivated areas such as farmland.

The Common Crane is omnivorous and eats a wide assortment of plant and animal matter. It enjoys berries, especially cranberries, roots, leaves, as well as insects, small birds, and small mammals.

Common Cranes in Flight (Photo by Andreas Trepte, *www.photo-natur.de*.)

Common Cuckoo (Cuculus canorus)
(32 cm.) Upperparts grey with black tail; black bars in white abdomen; yellow iris; unbarred rump

The Common Cuckoo is a member of a notorious family of the birds, "Cuculidae," the cuckoos. Cuckoos also have an order named after them, "Cuculiformes," which includes roadrunners, anis and coucals. Their position in an order other than Passeriformes means that despite a similar appearance, cuckoos are not considered "songbirds".

All species of cuckoos derive their names from the call of the male Common Cuckoo which is heard during summer in the Common Cuckoo's breeding range. During the summer breeding period, this species utters a loud and clear "kuk-oo" refrain from the treetops. The name "cuckoo" in English, is an excellent example of onomatopoeia being applied in the name of a bird.
Cuckoos of all species have earned their notorious reputations due to their practice of "brood parasitism." The females of cuckoo species do not make nests nor possess any desire to raise their own chicks. Instead, they lay their eggs in the nests of other, usually smaller, birds and in so doing force their parental duties on them. Female cuckoos do so by visiting nests, pushing an egg out of those nests, and leaving one of their own. They will visit many nests and repeat the process. The Common Cuckoo is particular about which species it will victimize with its parasitic behavior, preferring to inconvenience the females of the reed warbler group.

In addition to their shirking of parental responsibilities, cuckoos' reputations have been further sullied by their occasion habit of eating the eggs and chicks of other bird species.

Also known at times as the Eurasian Cuckoo, the Common Cuckoo breeds in Europe and Asia, and can be found in winter in Africa and Southeast Asia. In China, it breeds in every part of the country except the western desert regions where it is never seen. It prefers to live in open wooded areas.

In addition to the occasional egg and chick the Common Cuckoo's diet consists of insects, particularly species of hairy caterpillars which other birds avoid. It would be considered an insectivore as it rarely eats food from other sources.

Although the Common Cuckoo does possess some habits that we might describe as despicable, this bird is nonetheless an interesting creature which although common, is rarely seen.

Common Cuckoo (Photo by Steve Garvie)

Common Hoopoe (Upupa epops)
(25-30cm.) Long bill, large frilled crest, brown head, chest and back, black and white striped wings and tail.

The Common Hoopoe is perhaps the most unique and interesting bird in China. Its odd name is the phonic transcription of the sound of its voice. It is another widespread species that is found throughout much of Eurasia and Africa. It is one of the few species of birds in the world that does not have other close relatives among the bird world.

Not only does the hoopoe have a unique genus and species, this single species belongs its own family as well. Most bird species have close cousins who share its genus and family. The hoopoe's status as a sole species in the family, "Upupidae," makes it a bird of particular interest.

The hoopoe is instantly recognizable and unmistakable and is a pleasing bird to watch. The hoopoe could only possibly be confused with a woodpecker, a type of bird it is distantly related to, but its curved, thin bill instantly distinguishes it from the woodpecker clan.

The hoopoe is a well-loved species throughout its range due to its consumption of many insects that are considered crop damaging pests such as grasshoppers and locusts. Due to this fact, many countries have set up protective measures to ensure its survival. It will also eat small vertebrates such as lizards and frogs. The hoopoe feeds by probing the ground with its long sensitive bill and extracting tasty morsels.

Throughout its range, the hoopoe is population is strong. In China, the hoopoe is also doing well and is fairly common. However, the hoopoe is not so common that it is often seen on city streets and parks, so seeing one is always a treat.
The hoopoe has an undulating flight much like the movement of an amusement park roller coaster. Upon alighting on a perch and when alarmed, the hoopoe flashes its frilled head crest.
The hoopoe has achieved legendary status in many old world cultures around the world. In ancient Egypt and Minoa, it was depicted on temple walls. In ancient Greece, it was credited as the "King of Birds" in literary works. It is the national bird of Israel, and deserves greater recognition in China.

Common Hoopoe (Photo by Brian Westland)

Common Kestrel (Falco columbarius)
(33 cm.) Long grey tail, black pointed wings, streaked belly

The Common Kestrel is a "raptor" or "bird of prey," one of those species of birds that hunts small animals and kills them with special adaptations designed specifically for killing. It is a member of a family of small raptors, "Falconidae," the falcons. All falcons are swift and skilled fliers with pointed wings and long tails which allow these birds to reach high speeds of flight. One North American species, the Peregrine Falcon, is credited as being the fastest animal in the world, being able to exceed 200 km/hour in a dive.

The Common Kestrel, while not as fast as the Peregrine Falcon, is one of the most skilled aerialists in the bird world. It is a wonder to behold as it hovers and dives in its hunts for small rodents in the open habitat it loves. This bird is often seen perched in dead trees and atop telephone poles on roadsides.

This species is semi-cosmopolitan and can be found in Africa, Europe and Asia. It has even been reported as a vagrant visitor to the East Coast of North America. In China, this bird is a year-long resident throughout most of China except the western desert regions.

The Common Kestrel is an early spring breeder that nests in the cavities of trees or buildings. Often, they will also use the old nest of a crow or magpie. The female lays 3-6 eggs and incubates them for about one month before hatching. The female alone will attend to the eggs, leaving the male to hunt and supply food. Once the eggs have hatched, both male and female will attend to the hunting of prey and feeding of the chicks.

This species will consume a wide variety of animal matter depending on the season. Mice, voles and shrews seem to be the preferred diet, but other vertebrates such as bats, frogs and lizards and small songbirds will also be taken. Many kinds of insects are also enjoyed, especially large ones such as beetles and grasshoppers.

The Common Kestrel is a beautiful and fascinating raptor that should known to all.

Common Kestrel (Photo by Andreas Trepte, www.photo-natur.de)

Common Kingfisher (Alcedo atthis)
Field marks: Green; wings and head; orange belly; blue back; long bill.'

The common kingfisher is one of the smallest and most common of the kingfisher family, "Alcedinidae." It is a widespread species that can be found across Europe and Asia, and in winter, Africa and South Asia as far as Borneo and Java.

In China, it is a non-migratory species that will live year round in most places that can offer open fresh water from which the kingfisher can hunt for fish small aquatic animals. The common kingfisher will migrate from the northern part of its breeding range to southern points of the breeding range that offer unfrozen fresh water in winter.

The kingfisher gets its name from its mode of acquiring food, fishing. All kingfishers hunt for fish and small freshwater animals in lakes and ponds. All kingfishers are armed with long, dagger-like bills with which they grab or impale their prey. The birds will perch on rocks or branches of trees which overhang the surface of a lake or pond and wait until they spot their prey. They bob their heads while searching the water surface for prey. When a potential meal is spotted, they will leap from their perch and dive straight into the water to seize their prize. At other times, kingfishers hover above the water's surface and dive when prey is spotted.

To sit quietly at a pond's edge and watch the antics of kingfishers as they engage in their fishing activities is among the finest scenarios in birding.

The present species is particularly active in its fishing attempts diving frequently and flying about to find alternative perches. The common kingfisher flies low across the water and its wings make a noticeable whirring noise in flight.

Because the species' survival is so closely linked to water, the common kingfisher nests in holes found on riverbanks or the sides of ponds. This close proximity to their hunting grounds helps to ensure the survival of young chicks.

Young kingfishers must learn quickly to fish and must be afforded enough time to observe the parents' fishing skills. Often, young kingfishers do not acquire these skills fast enough are forced to fend for themselves before they are ready to do so. Inevitably, many young kingfishers do not survive their year. Also, many young kingfishers do not survive their first few attempts at diving. Some drown when they fail to exit the water fast enough and their feathers become waterlogged.

Common Kingfisher (Photo by Andreas Trepte, *www.photo-natur.de*)

Common Merganser (Mergus merganser)
(68 cm.) Male: Large; long, thin hooked bill; greenish-black head and back; white under parts. Female/immature male: Dark grey upper parts; pale grey under parts; brown head; white chin

The Common Merganser, also known as the "Goosander," is a member of the family of ducks, geese, and swans and is also a member of the subfamily, "Merginae," the mergansers. All mergansers are also known as "fish ducks," as they are fish-hunting ducks which have serrated bills which allow them to grip their slippery prey. Their unique bills also provide them with the nickname, "sawbills."

The Common Merganser bears a superficial resemblance to a Mallard with its greenish-black head, but its red, serrated bill, larger size and black and white body distinguish it easily. As with many other bird species, the male of this species is decidedly more beautiful than the female. The female of this species has a brown head, grey body and duller red bill.

The Common Merganser is found throughout the Northern Hemisphere. In China, it breeds in the northeast and the northwest and winters in the southeast. In the breeding season it can be found in lakes and rivers in wooded areas.

As it is a cavity nester, the Common Merganser requires mature stands of trees from which to find a nest hole, and it shows a preference for abandoned woodpecker nests. In areas with no trees, this species will find holes in cliffs and high riverbanks. The female lays a large clutch of eggs, usually 10-12 in number. Immediately after hatching, the chicks are taken in their mother's bill to a lake or river where they can begin feeding.

In addition to fish, Common Mergansers feed on other aquatic animals such as crustaceans, insect larvae, mollusks, and even amphibians. All mergansers are diving ducks that plunge to often great depths in the pursuit of prey.

The Common Merganser is partially-migratory and will only leave the parts of its breeding range where open water freezes. In China, this means that the birds are absent during winter in all locations north of around Shandong province.

Common Merganser (Photo by Tony Hisgett)

Common Moorhen (Gallinula chloropus)
(31 cm.) Black; red frontal shield; short bill; line of white streaks across flanks; two white patches under tail

The Common Moorhen is an unmistakable member of the rail family, "Rallidae." It is a large species of rail, and it is far more conspicuous than many members of its family. Rails are generally skulking birds of swamps which hide deep within tall stands of reeds. The Common Moorhen makes its presence far more obvious by noisily walking on pond and swamp vegetation or swimming out in open water like a duck. The bird gets its name from the old English word, "moor" which means marsh or swamp. In North America, it is called the "Common Gallinule."

This species is very attractive in its uniformly slate black plumage with white streaks on its flanks. The legs and feet of the bird are yellow. The bill is green with a red base that extends up the bird's face to form a noticeable and odd-looking frontal shield. The species displays a persistent habit of flicking its tail.
The bird is another extremely widespread and common species that is found throughout most of the world. It is not found in polar regions, or throughout much

of the tropics. Throughout its range, this species lives in lakes, ponds, and swamps which offer ample open water.

The Common Moorhen is another omnivorous species that will consume a large variety of foods. It feeds on various aquatic vegetation and aquatic creatures.

This species will generally breed in early spring in most of its breeding range. The female moorhen builds a basket-like nest on the ground among the thick vegetation and lays around 8 eggs. Both parents share the duties of incubating the eggs and the feeding of young chicks after hatching.

There are many subspecies of this bird in China, and there are some differences in the appearance of these subspecies. The males of all subspecies, however, are easily identifiable as Common Pheasants. All have the signature mottled brown body, greenish-black head and red orbital skin on the face. The males of most subspecies have a white neck ring. The females of all subspecies are dull-looking brown birds which are easily confused with females of other pheasant species.

The Common Pheasant is found throughout the eastern half of China where it is a non-migratory, resident species. As this bird tends to stay close to the ground among thick vegetation, it is more often heard than seen. Its call is a two part, loud coughing which is followed by an audible whir of the bird's wings.

The Common Pheasant prefers grasslands near water, but it is extremely adaptable and can live in woodlands, marshlands and cultivated areas, also. The males of all pheasant species are polygamous and possess harems of females with which they breed. The Common Pheasant nests on the ground and the female lays a large clutch of usually around ten eggs.

This species is omnivorous and will feed on seeds, fruits, insects, and even vertebrates such as lizards, snakes, and even small mammals and other birds.

Common Pheasant (Photo by Lukasz Lukasik)

Common Snipe (Gallinago gallinago)
(26 cm.) Long thin bill; stripes on face; eye stripe; dark brown streaked upperparts; light brown streaked underparts; very erratic flight; noisy, calls often in alarm.

The Common Snipe is a common bird in China which is rarely seen and little known. Its lack of fame can be attributed to its elusive lifestyle and seeming complete lack of comfort in the presence of humans.

When this bird is disturbed by human presence, it will sit motionless blending in with its surroundings with its well-camouflaged plumage. If approached too closely, it will fly off while delivering a distinctive "snape, snape" call. It flies off when flushed in a strange zig-zag pattern which is a defense to confuse predators. It is usually when this bird is flying away that the human observer first has a chance to take notice of it. Only birdwatchers that are specifically looking for this bird will likely get a chance to properly observe one.

The Common Snipe is a member of the family, "Scolopacidae," a very large family of birds that are similar to snipes such as sandpipers, curlews, stints and tattlers. All members of this family have long legs, pointed wings and long bills. Usually these birds are found on beaches, mudflats, or in shallow rivers where they use their long bills to probe for aquatic animals.

The Common Snipe's diet consists largely of earthworms and insects which they probe for with their long bills in the marshes and bogs which constitute their favorite habitats. During migration, they can be found in city parks which offer the swampy conditions they like.

During the breeding season, the male snipe attracts a mate by flying high in the sky in a circular fashion and then diving, which produces a goat-like squeal as wind rushes through the snipe's tail feathers. This elaborate display is called, winnowing". The Common Snipe's name in many languages around the world translates as "flying goat."

The female lays four eggs in a well-hidden nest on the ground. When the eggs hatch, the snipe chicks are cared for by both parents. Like other members of the Scolopacidae family, snipe chicks develop and achieve independence quickly.

Common Snipe (Photo by Sean Breazeal)

Common Stonechat (Saxicola maurus)
(14 cm.) Male: Black head; dark brown back; white patches on neck and wings; whitish rump; brown breast. Female: Duller than male; no black; light brown under parts; white patch on wing

The Common Stonechat, also known as the Siberian Stonechat, is a bird that has been recently reclassified by ornithologists and placed in a new family. Once considered a thrush, it has been now placed in the family, Muscicapidae, the family of flycatchers. Several sub-species of this bird can be found in Europe and Asia.

The bird derives its name from its voice which has been likened to the sound of two stones being struck together. This species is strict insectivore, like other members of the flycatcher family. It prefers open scrubby habitat where it can find low bushes in which it likes to perch and wait for its insect prey.

The Common Stonechat has a wide breeding range which covers most of temperate Asia. In China, its breeding range includes the northeast and central parts of the country. It generally only inhabits the East Coast of the country during its spring and fall migrations.

This bird seems particularly averse to cool temperatures and its northern breeding range and departs these regions as early as possible to avoid the rapid drop in temperature that can happen at these latitudes in early fall. Stonechats which breed in warmer regions usually do not migrate. If the breeding site of a Common Stonechat is warm come fall and winter, there will likely be no southward movement.

The Common Stonechat is indeed a common and widespread species that can fairly reliably be spotted in eastern China during its migrations in spring and fall.

Common Stonechat (Photo by Jose Sousa)

Common Tern (Sterna hirundo)
Field marks: (35 cm.) White and grey; black head cap; long bill.

Terns are often easily confused with gulls. Both terns and gulls are sea birds which are usually found along the coastlines of most countries. Both types of bird are largely white with long bills and similar black markings. A first time observer of a tern could easily be forgiven for confusing one of these birds for a gull. There are some fundamental differences between gulls and terns, though.

Terns are generally smaller than gulls with sharply pointed wings and deeply forked tails. Their bills come to a sharp point, whereas the bill of gull is rounded at the tip. Their legs are much shorter than a gull's leg. Like gulls, terns are hunters of fish, and they can often be seen hovering above the surface of lakes and seas preparing to dive in their attempts to capture prey.

Many terns are highly-migratory. In fact, the world champion among the animal world for long migrations is the Arctic Tern, a North American species which migrates between the North and South poles, a distance of 20, 000 km., twice a year.

The Common Tern is also well traveled, moving between their breeding grounds in northern China and wintering grounds in Southeast Asia. Common Terns are very nearly cosmopolitan and can be found throughout much of the Northern Hemisphere.

The Common Tern will breed in colonies that can exceed 5000 mated pairs of birds. They nest on the ground in freshwater and saltwater environments from coastal sea locations to freshwater lakes. They are quite adaptable and can use human structures as nesting sites as well. The female usually lays three eggs and will be very aggressive in protecting eggs and chicks. They have been known to attack humans who venture too close to their nests.

Common Tern (Photo by Joby Joseph)

Crested Mynah (Acridotheres cristatellus)
(26 cm.) All black; prominent crest; white patches in wings easily seen in flight

The Crested Mynah is a large member of the starling family, "Sturnidae." It is the only mynah species which can be found in the temperate portion of China. Other mynah species are birds of the tropics, requiring the hot temperatures that these latitudes provide. The small flocks of Crested Mynahs this writer sees in Qingdao's parks may be the northernmost colony of this species in the country.

This species gets its name from its prominent crest, a feature which other Asian mynah species lack. Its uniformly black plumage and conspicuous white wing patches are also signature characteristics.

Many birds of this species are trapped and sold on the caged bird market in this country. They are popular cage birds due to their unique vocal abilities including a talent for mimicry. Caged birds can be taught to speak human words without little difficulty. Of course, the birds cannot understand the meanings of the words they speak, but their human owners enjoy listening to them, anyway. In nature, mynahs will imitate the calls of other bird species.
The Crested Mynah is a bird of open country such as farmland, field, and pasture. Its love of this habitat makes it an ideal urban dweller. City parks and gardens offer this bird just this kind of habitat.

This bird, like all members of the starling family, is an omnivore which will subsist on primarily fruits, insects and other small invertebrates. This species will usually be found strutting on the ground in search of food in parks and gardens in urban areas.

Crested Mynah (Photo by Charles Lam)

Daurian Redstart (Phoenicurus auroreus)
(15 cm.) Field marks: Male: White wing patch, rusty breast and belly, black wings and throat. Female: Uniformly dull brown; white patch on wing.

The Daurian Redstart, named after a part of Siberia in Russia is a small and active bird of the family, "Muscicapidae." It is normally only seen in much of Eastern China during the fall and winter months when it has completed its fall migration from its breeding grounds in northern China and Russia.

The male of the species is very attractive indeed with its rusty breast and belly contrasting with the black of the face, throat and back. The female is much duller with a uniformly brown body. Both males and females have bold white patches on the wings, which is a key identifying mark. This stark contrast in appearance with males possessing more beautiful plumage than females is common in songbirds worldwide and is known as, "sexual dimorphism."

The Daurian Redstart is a common and successful species that graces parks, gardens and roadsides throughout South Central China every winter. During its summer breeding season this species prefers open forests and the edges of agricultural lands.

The Daurian Redstart, like other members of the redstart family, is not a shy bird and will usually allow the human observer to approach at fairly close range before it flies off.

The Daurian Redstart is another omnivorous species that eats insects, berries and seeds. It can often be observed flicking its tail excitedly while perched and on the lookout for a meal.

Daurian Redstart (Photo by Alder Chang)

Dollarbird (Eurystomus orientalis) Sanbaoniao
(30 cm.) Large, slightly hooked red bill; large head; bluish-green plumage; light patches in wings seen in flight

The Dollarbird, also known as the Oriental Dollarbird, is a member of the roller family, "Coraciiformes," and is the only member of this family of birds that can be found in East China. The Dollarbird gets its name from the blue spots seen in its wings during flight. The spots look vaguely like coins of money.

The Dollarbird is a large attractive species of roller with green and blue plumage and a large red bill. The bill of young birds is dark and gradually becomes red with age. The large red bill is somewhat hooked, giving it a slight resemblance to a bird of prey. The Dollarbird is often attacked by small songbirds that mistake it for a predatory bird.

This species is found throughout Eastern China during the summer breeding season. While it is a widespread species, it is in no place a common bird, so the sighting of a Dollarbird is always an occasion to be celebrated and savored.

The Dollarbird will often be first seen as it perches, flycatcher-style, in the exposed branch of a dead tree, waiting for insects to fly by. This species is a strict insectivore, and as such it must migrate to warm climates in the winter where a steady supply of insects is assured.

The Dollarbird is migratory only in the parts of its range that become cold in winter and will not support insect life. In the warmer parts of its range, the Dollarbird will set up year-round residence.

Dollarbird (Photo by Dick Daniels)

Dusky Thrush (Turdus eunomos)
(25 cm.) Heavily-patterned black and white; reddish-brown wing linings; broad reddish-brown wing patch.

The Dusky Thrush is a member of a large family of sweet-singing songbirds, the thrushes, of the family, "Turdidae." Thrushes throughout the world are considered among the most gifted of avian singers for their beautiful, rich flute-like warblings. Many thrush species in China are also gifted musical performers, with the Song Thrush as perhaps the most gifted of the clan.

The Dusky Thrush is also quite musical, performing its simple whistled song many times from the time it sets off on its spring migration north through the breeding season in mid- summer.

Thrushes and other species of songbirds sing not only to attract a mate, but also to set up territories during the annual summer breeding season. Each pair of birds of a particular species needs several square kilometers of space in a particular location from which they build nests and have exclusive food-gathering rights. The maintenance of strict territories ensures that chicks raised by parent birds of a particular species will have access to the necessary food resources for their survival.

The Dusky Thrush's song is less often heard in China, however, as its breeding range is in the Far North of Russia. This bird seeks out grassy fields, pastures, and similar open country with scattered trees as its preferred habitat. The female lays 3-5 eggs in a rather messy-looking nest.

Following the breeding season, Dusky Thrushes will migrate south and spend the winters in Central and Southern China and Southeast Asia. It is during the winter that the Chinese observer will most often have the opportunity to glimpse this handsome bird in city parks. This bird is quite common and can be readily found in southeast China during the winter months.

The Dusky Thrush is another versatile omnivore that is fond of insects, especially mosquitoes, and berries.

Dusky Thrush (Photo by Richard Fisher)

Eurasian Blackbird (Turdus merula)
(29 cm.) Entirely black plumage; yellow bill and eye ring.

The Eurasian Blackbird, often referred to as the "Common Blackbird" is a very common member of the thrush family, "Turdidae." Like many other birds in this family, the male Eurasian Blackbird is a talented singer that serenades females and threatens other males with its melodious singing during the spring and summer.

Despite bearing the name, "blackbird," it should be noted that this bird is a true thrush and is not related to members of the American blackbird family, "Icteridae." As one of the few completely black species of songbirds in Europe and Asia, the bird's English name is understandable, nonetheless. The male has uniformly black plumage with a striking yellow eye-ring and yellow bill. The female is a less attractive mix of black and brown, but still possesses the yellow bill, which is this species' diagnostic field mark.

The Eurasian Blackbird is found throughout South and Central China as far north as Shandong province. It is not a migratory species and can be found year-round in most part of its range. In the northern part of its range, some birds may wander south during winter to seek out better environmental conditions. It is generally a hardy species, however.

This bird is a common sight in city parks and gardens or any place that offers it its preferred foods, earthworms, insects, and other small invertebrates. It is a versatile omnivore that also enjoys berries and fruits.

During the summer breeding season, the male Eurasian Blackbird will attract a mate with a strange courtship display of running and head-bobbing. After mating, the couple will build a cup-shaped nest made of mud, grass and other vegetation.

The female lays 3-5 eggs and incubates them herself for about two weeks. Due to the accessible position of Eurasian Blackbird nests, predators often take eggs and chicks. Despite this, this species continues to maintain a large population, and this bird continues to be regular attraction in city parks in all major Chinese cities from Qingdao in the north all the way down the East Coast of China.

Eurasian Blackbird (Photo by Brian Westland)

Eurasian Jay (Garrulus glandarius)
(35 cm.) Pinkish color; white throat; black "mustache"; blue and black pattered wings; white rump

The Eurasian Jay, like other jays found in the world, is part of the "Corvidae" family which includes crows and magpies. The Eurasian Jay shares many characteristics of these birds including a harsh voice, exceptional intelligence and a somewhat dark reputation for aggressive and predatory behavior.

This species shares the Black-billed Magpie's love of eggs, and it will actively seek out the nests of other bird species from which to steal eggs and even chicks. Its aggressive nature is most often directed at birds larger than itself, however.

The Eurasian Jay is known as the fierce nemesis of several birds of prey. It will harass owls and hawks during the day in an attempt to protect its own kind. During its attacks on the Tawny Owl, the Eurasian Jay will mimic the call of the owl. This bird has a great gift of mimicry, and its imitations of the sounds of other birds are difficult to distinguish from the actual calls of the species it imitates.

In addition to eggs, the Eurasian Jay eats seeds, berries and other fruits. It is especially fond of acorns, and it seeks out oak forests as habitat to give it a steady supply of this food. Various animals such as small animals, insects, and other birds constitute a significant part of its diet.

This is a widespread species which is found throughout Europe, the Middle East, and Asia. In China, this species is found in most of the eastern half of the country. Like most members of the Corvidae family, it is a non-migratory resident species within its range. Its varied diet allows it to consume foods during any season throughout the year.

Perhaps due to the destruction of the mixed oak forests which it favors, this species is moving into the cities where urban parkland can offer it the conditions it needs to survive.

The Eurasian Jay nests in a large shrub or a tree, and the female lays 4-6 eggs in an untidy stick nest. Both parents will feed the chicks after the eggs have hatched.

Despite its aggressive personality, or perhaps due to it, this species can end up being a prey item at night for the species of raptors with which it battles during the day.

Euasian Jay (Photo by Pawel Kuzniar)

Eurasian Nuthatch (Sitta europaea)
(13 cm.) Large head; short tail; grey upperparts; whitish-brown underparts; black eye line

The Eurasian Nuthatch belongs to a family of small, interesting and rather odd birds, "Sittidae," the nuthatches. The name, "nuthatch" is derived from their habit of drilling acorns and nuts into the trunks of trees where they can be opened by "hacking" them with their bills. All nuthatches have very large heads, short tails, and powerful feet and claws for gripping trees.

Nuthatches are usually seen climbing along the branches and trunks of trees like a woodpecker; however, they often climb down a tree headfirst which is something a woodpecker would never attempt.

The Eurasian Nuthatch is the most common and widespread of the nuthatch family. It is sometimes simply referred to as "the nuthatch" due to its familiarity with bird-lovers and status as sole present member of its family throughout much of Europe. This species is found throughout Europe and Asia, except Ireland. In China, it is a common bird in many parts of its range which is limited to the eastern half of the country.

This species is found in deciduous forests where it can find the acorns and nuts which it so loves. It also consumes insects which it finds during its foraging missions along the trunks and branches of deciduous trees. At times, this bird will feed on the ground. During winter, the Eurasian Nuthatch will visit feeding stations that offer seeds, often bullying other bird species that they may encounter there. Due to its varied diet that is not solely dependant on insects, this species is non-migratory, and like other non-migratory bird species, its fall and winter wanderings will only be motivated by winter food shortages in its summer range.

The Eurasian Nuthatch nests in a hole or crevice that is lined with grass or tree bark. The female will deposit 5-8 eggs in the nest.

This species is quite noisy, and can often be heard to repeat its trademark call, the loud and sharp, "twet, twet, twet" At other times it can be heard to whistle a rather melodious song. It is, after all, despite its rather strange appearance, a songbird.

Eurasian Nuthatch (Photo by Luc Viatour www.Lucnix.be)

Eurasian Siskin (Carduelis spinus) Huang que

(11.5 cm.) Very small; short bill; banded yellow and black wings; adult male has black cap and chin and yellow on head, rump and base of tail. Female: Duller; more streaked than male; lacking a black cap and chin.

The Eurasian Siskin is a very small and very active member of the finch family, "Fringillidae". It also qualifies in the category of "winter finch," as it is part of a group of finches that breed in extreme nortern latitudes and generally only visit southern temperate regions during the winter months. All winter finches, including crossbills, siskins and others follow several-year cycles of migration in which they are absent in southern regions for several years and then appear in great numbers during one year. These irregular migration patterns are directly related to climatic changes and variable food supplies.

The range of the Eurasian Siskin is separated into two sections through Eurasia. One part is in North Europe with the other in North Asia. It is absent from the portion of Russia that separates these two sections. Its summer breeding range includes the extreme northeast of Heilongjiang Province up into Russia. During the winters that it chooses to seek southern climes, it can be found throughout much of Eastern China as far south as Shenzhen and Hong Kong.

Like other winter finches, the Eurasian Siskin is a largely a seed eater which can survive without difficulty at northern latitudes where coniferous forests offer seeds all year long.
This species is almost always seen feeding high in the trees as it rarely ventures close to the ground. It is quite acrobatic in its search for food, often hanging upside down in the manner of a tit.

During those winters when it ventures south to temperate regions, it will feed from seeds of both coniferous and deciduous trees. In summer, this bird will feed its chicks insects, as the proteins found in animal matter will allow for faster development of their young.

During the winter, males and females form pairs that will mate in the coming spring. The birds construct a nest high in the upper branches of coniferous tree, usually a pine. The female lays 2-6 eggs and incubates them herself. The chicks are "nidiculous,' meaning that they remain close to their nests long after hatching remaining dependant on their parents for food.

Eurasian Siskin (Photo by Slawek Staszczuk)

Eurasian Skylark (Alauda jaopica) Yunque
(18 cm.) Erectile crest; mottled grayish-brown with streaking; shorter legs and than other larks; tail is forked with white edges; stands less upright than other larks

The Eurasian Skylark, often referred to simply as, "Skylark", is one of the great performers of the animal kingdom. It is not much to look at, with its rather dull plumage of mottled grey and brown, but it performs one of the greatest courtship displays of any animal. All larks constitute the family, "Alaudidae".

Larks look similar to pipits, but have thicker bills, shorter tails, and many, including the Eurasian Lark, have short, erectile crests. Many larks sing while they are in flight. The English expression, "on a lark', means to have a good time, and certainly the birds of this family seem to be enjoying themselves much of the time. All larks are fine warbling singers, and one Chinese lark, the Mongolian Lark, is a favorite cage bird in the China for its lovely song.

In China, the Eurasian Lark breeds in summer in "dongbei" and winters throughout the rest of the eastern portion of the country. This is a very common species in the northern parts of the country in winter.

The Eurasian Skylark inhabits open grassy places such as grasslands, marshes and farmland. These habitats provide this bird with the insects and seeds that constitute its diet. This bird spends much of its time on the ground foraging for its favorite food.

The male Eurasian Skylark really comes to life when it leaves the ground during the breeding season. Although it has an erratic mode of flight, this bird often flies to extremely high altitudes where the bird is barely visible in the sky to perform flying/singing show of epic proportions. From a height of around 100 metres the male bird begins a two to three minute song which is accompanied by daring acrobatics in the air. While in mid song the males dive, hover and flutter, finally diving back to the ground at suicidal speed.

Females Skylarks, watching from the ground, will choose a male based on the length and quality of the performance. After mating, the pair will make a grass nest on the ground and the female will deposit her three eggs.

Eurasian Skylark (Photo by Alpsdake)

Eurasian Tree Sparrow (Passer Montanus)

(12-14 cm.) Brown and white plumage, black throat cheek spot, reddish-brown crown.

The Eurasian Tree Sparrow is one of the most familiar birds in Eastern China. It is found in every part of China, and it is the ubiquitous brown bird that is found in every city in the eastern half of the country. In Western China, a similar species, the House Sparrow, is its ubiquitous city-dwelling counterpart. Like other birds with thick conical bills adapted for seed eating, it is a member of the finch family, "Passeridae." The members of this family that carry the name, "sparrow," are distinct from North American sparrows.

This bird is familiar to everyone in eastern China, and it is often just referred to as "sparrow" or "maque." Those who are familiar with this species are probably unaware that it is not the only sparrow in the country. In fact, China has 12 sparrow species. However, besides this species counterpart, the House Sparrow, in the West, other sparrow species will rarely be encountered by Chinese city-dwellers.

The Eurasian Tree Sparrow is another omnivorous species that feeds by foraging on the ground for seeds and grains. In the summer breeding season, it will also partake of insects, millipedes, centipedes, and spiders.

This species should be appreciated despite its over-familiarity for its attractive appearance and the ease with which it keeps company with humans. In many places in China, however, this species is considered an enemy of the grain farmer as vast flocks of this bird can inflict significant damage to grain crops. Mao Zi Dong famously attempted to eradicate this species in 1958 in order to save grain supplies. However, after initial success, many grain consuming insects on which the sparrows feed inflicted worse damage in the sparrows' absence.

The Eurasian Tree Sparrow is a tree cavity nesting species that can also use a rock face containing a cavity as well. A female sparrow will typically lay 5-6 eggs. Young sparrows need up to a year to achieve fully independence.

Before the advent of human civilization and the growth of cities, this species favored lightly wooded, open country. The birds still exist in these places, but urbanization has created city paradises for these birds to conquer.

Eurasian Tree Sparrow (Photo by Yiwen Yiwen)

Eurasian Wryneck (Jynx torquilla)
(17 cm.) White eye line over brown eye line; grayish-brown head and back; heavily barred whitish underparts; often twists neck from side to side.

The Eurasian Wryneck is one of the oddest birds in China. It has a bizarre, even alien air about it.   It is a member of the woodpecker family, "picidae," but it does not behave like a woodpecker. It seems to be more the avian equivalent of an anteater, that odd, strangely shaped mammal that eats ants exclusively and laps them up with a long, sticky tongue.

Most woodpeckers conform to a standard mode of behavior-climb around on the trunk of a tree and probe for insects that can be found in the bark. If none can be found, drill holes in the tree and extract the insects that way. The wryneck rejects this established behavior and chooses instead to hunt on the ground for its favorite food, ants, in a most un-woodpecker-like manner. The Eurasian Wryneck gets its name from its habit of twisting its neck from side to side when it is alarmed.

The Eurasian Wryneck is another semi-cosmopolitan bird species that can be found in Europe and Asia, and in winter in Africa. In China, the Eurasian Wryneck can be found   in the northeast in summer, through the central East Coast during spring and fall and in the southeast in winter.

If a female Eurasian Wryneck is disturbed while at its nest, it will engage in its head-twisting behavior accompanied with loud hissing noises. This odd behavior was noticed by some in Europe who practiced witchcraft and the bird was often used in rituals. Part of the bird's Latin name, "jynx," means to put an evil spell on someone, more often spelled "jinx" in English.

Like other woodpeckers, the Eurasian Wryneck nests in the cavity of a tree. This species, lacking the powerful bill and adaptations for drilling that other woodpeckers possess, will not make its own hole, instead it will find abandoned cavities left by other woodpeckers.

The Eurasian Wryneck's appearance is just as strange as its curious habits. It looks unlike any other bird. Its long heavily barred and mottled body gives it a rather reptilian feel. For all its strangeness, this species must be appreciated its uniqueness, for it is truly just one of a kind.

Eurasian Wryneck (Photo by Martien Brand)

Great Cormorant (Phalacrocorax carbo) Putong luci
(90 cm.) Large; glossy black; thick bill; white throat and cheeks.

The Great Cormorant is the largest member of the "phalacrocoracidae" family in China. All members of this family are fish-eating species of birds with long, sharply-hooked bills. Cormorants, especially this species, have had a long and close history with people in China. For many centuries, Chinese fishermen have trained these birds to assist them in their fish-gathering activities.

The Great Cormorant is a very common and widespread species that is found worldwide, only missing in a few locations such as the western part of North America. As it is a fish-eating bird, it will be found in aquatic habitats such as oceans, estuaries, and freshwater lakes and rivers. In winter, it will migrate from northern latitudes where water freezes and head to coastal areas where it can find unfrozen water.

The Great Cormorant breeds in coastal areas and inland areas which are close to the coast. The female lays 3-4 eggs in a nest of seaweed or sticks which is usually situated in a tree or n a cliff.

If needed, this species can dive to great depth in its pursuit of fish, but often deep dives are not necessary as this bird is often found fishing in shallow water. Cormorants are often seen perched on rocks beside water with their wings outstretched to the sun. Unlike many aquatic species of birds like ducks and geese, cormorants lack the water resistant oil in their feathers that other aquatic species possess. During their hunts, the feathers of these birds become water-logged and significant time is needed in the sun's warmth to dry them

In China, Japan, and several other locations in the world, Cormorant fishing has been practiced for many years. Fishermen used to see the cormorant as a competitor that could deplete fish stocks, so many decided to employ the bird in the service of humans. By tying a line around the cormorants necks, tight enough to prevent swallowing, fishermen could place several birds on a line and reel them into their boats when the birds have had time enough in the water to catch fish. After the birds have been pulled back in the boat, the fishermen can extract the fish from the birds' by forcing their bills open.

Great Cormorant (Photo by Andreas Trepte)

Great Crested Grebe (Podiceps cristatus) Fengtou piti
(50 cm.) Large; slender neck; conspicuous dark crest; whitish underparts; grayish-brown upperparts.

The Great Crested Grebe is a largest member of the grebe family, "Podicipedidae" found in China. It is about twice the size of the smallest Chinese grebe, the Little Grebe.   It is a handsome waterbird named for the prominent tufts of feathers on the head.

This bird is widespread through China and is found everywhere in the country at some time of year except for the extreme tip of "dongbei" and the western desert regions. In the breeding season it is found throughout the northern half of the country. In winter, it is found along the East Coast from around Dalian south to Hong Kong and inland through most of the southeast.

The Great Crested Grebe can be found in freshwater lakes during the summer breeding season and in freshwater and saltwater environments, especially along the seasides of eastern China in winter.

Like other grebes, this species feeds primarily on fish, but it will also eat crustaceans, insects and frogs. It is capable of deep dives underwater to pursue fish and other aquatic creatures.

All grebes are supremely adapted for life in the water which makes them ill equipped to move on land. For example, a grebe's legs are set far back near the rump. This adaptation aids in swimming, but makes walking on land a near impossibility. All grebes nest directly beside water to avoid the necessity of land movement.

Several grebe species have elaborate courtship displays, and the Great Crested Grebe is no exception. In the freshwater lakes of their summer breeding grounds, these birds put on a dance performance of great artistry. A pair of birds face each other and lift their bodies out of the water while nodding their heads up and down, often while holding vegetation in their bills.

A typical brood consists of two eggs. When the chicks hatch, each parent will identify a favorite chick and take sole responsibility for the raising that chick

Great Crested Grebe (Photo by Andreas Trepte)

Great Spotted Woodpecker (Dendrocopos major)
  (24 cm.) Large black and white, white cheek, red head spot.

The Great Spotted Woodpecker is a member of the family, "picidae", the woodpeckers. Like all woodpeckers, it is usually found climbing around the trucks of large trees in a concentrated search for insects and their larvae. It is the most widespread woodpecker in China, and it is found throughout the East.

Both male and female Great Spotted Woodpeckers are "pied" meaning that they are primarily colored black and white. Both sexes have a pinkish-red vent, the area found under their tails. The male has a red spot on the back of its head that is missing in the female.

All woodpeckers have physical adaptations that allow them to lead their rather unconventional way of life. To allow them to grip tree bark, nature has provided them with two pairs of toes which point in opposite directions, allowing them to grip tree bark. Their unusually stiff tail feathers support them as they grip trees as well. They also have heavily reinforced skulls which can absorb the shocks they receive when heavily drilling holes in trees with their sharp beaks. The tongue of a woodpecker in extremely long allowing it to extend several centimeters from its bill, allowing the woodpecker to probe the holes it drills in trees for food.

The Great Spotted Woodpecker is a non-migratory resident throughout most of its Chinese range. It will sometimes venture south in winter from the coldest parts of its range. It is still a common winter bird in Beijing during winter, however.

This species is omnivorous; and although it is fond of insects, it will also consume eggs and chicks of other bird species, fruits, nuts, and seeds. It has even been known to eat small rodents.

The Great Spotted Woodpecker nests in an excavated tree cavity usually in a soft-wooded tree that is in some state of decay. The female lays 5-7 eggs and after hatching,   the chicks will gather at the hole entrance to clamber for food while the parent birds are absent on their food-finding missions.

Great Spotted Woodpecker (Photo by Maartin Visser)

Grey Heron (Ardea cinerea)
(95 cm.) Large, long bill and legs, grayish plumage

The Grey Heron is one of the largest members of the heron family, "Ardeidae", in China. It is a widespread species found in Africa and throughout temperate Europe and Asia. Only two other herons in China are of a similar size, the even larger and quite dark Purple Heron and the similarly sized, but all white, Great Egret. The greyish, yellow-billed Grey Heron is quite easy to distinguish from these other large members of its family.

Like all herons, egrets, and bitterns, this species flies with its head retracted to its body in an "s" shape, distinguishing it from other large flying waders such as storks and cranes.

The Grey Heron is a voracious eater armed with a lethal, dagger-like bill, and it wrecks havoc on the aquatic life of its watery habitat. It is not picky about the food it consumes and will snatch frogs, lizards, insects, fish, snakes, plovers, ducklings, and other small birds and their chicks. This species is usually a solitary hunter which will either stand in the shallow water of streams, lakes and ponds waiting motionless for prey to stray within striking range. They will also actively stalk other prey choices.

Like all herons, this species is a colony nester. It builds a solid and bulky nest of sticks which is situated in a tree close to the edge of a lake, marsh, or even a seaside.

The Grey Heron is described as locally common throughout its large range, meaning that in certain locations the bird may be uncommon or even rare, while in other places it is a common sight and easily found.

Grey Heron (Photo by JJ Harrison)

Grey Wagtail (Motacilla cinerea)
(19 cm.) Long tail; grey upperparts; grey head; white throat; yellow underparts; white eye line

The Grey Wagtail is a member of a small family of long, slender birds with long tails, the wagtails, "Moticillidae." These birds get their English names from their constant habit of "wagging" their tails. The Grey Wagtail is one of the most attractive members of the family with its lovely combination of grey head and back, black wings and yellow under parts.

This bird's range within China makes up the eastern half of the country with the breeding range in the "dongbei" region. In winter, it can be found throughout much of the southeast.

The Grey Wagtail is almost always found near water, especially rivers and streams. In summer in the north part of its range, it will nest very close to fast running rivers and streams, allowing the parent birds close proximity to their hunting grounds and growing chicks. This close proximity to both a food source and their nest helps ensure the survival of their chicks

This species is fond of small aquatic animals as food including flies, mayflies, crustaceans and mollusks. In winter, these birds have been known to return to exactly the same urban garden as past years.

This species, along with other wagtails are shy and difficult to approach if one wishes to observe this species it is often best to find a suitable location such as a park with a stream and wait quietly and inconspicuously for the birds to come to you.

Grey Wagtail (Photo by Brian Westland)

Grey-streaked Flycatcher (Muscicapa griseisticta)
(14 cm.) Small; grey upperparts; heavily streaked white underparts; eye ring

The Grey-streaked Flycatcher is a rather petite and slight member of the flycatcher family, but despite its diminutive size it engages in the pursuit of flying insects with all the fervor of other members of the flycatcher family.

This species is quite drab in appearance when compared with some other members of its family, but it is quite an attractive bird nonetheless. Unlike some other flycatcher species, males and females of this species look alike.

This species of flycatcher breeds in summer in the coniferous forests of northern China and Russia where it is especially fond of the Larch Tree for nesting. Like many other Chinese flycatchers, this bird embarks on a long-distance trek south along the Chinese East Coast to its wintering grounds. In winter, this species can be found in Taiwan, Borneo, Indonesia, the Philippines, and as far south as New Guinea.

The Grey-streaked Flycatcher can usually be found hunting for insects nearby rivers and streams as it seems to favor smaller insects such as mosquitoes that congregate near water.
This bird will perch patiently until potential prey is spotted, and then fly off quite a distance, often as far as 20 meters, in an attempt to capture a meal. The bird will return to exactly the same perch and begin the process again. More often than not, the flycatcher's attempts at capturing prey are successful.

All flycatchers are equipped with stiff bristles that surround the base of their bills. These bristles act as a net, assisting the flycatcher with the capture of its prey. All flycatcher species are also blessed with an extremely large gape (size of mouth with bill open) to further assist in their hunting activities.

Grey-streaked Flycatcher (Photo by Brian Westland)

Hwamei (Garrulax merulinus) Huamei
(22 cm.) Uniformly brown; white eye ring/eye line; yellow bill

The Hwamei is a bird which is familiar to most Chinese people. Few have seen it in its natural habitat, however. It is most often seen, unfortunately, in the cages which become the homes of many members of this species in China.

The Hwamei is a member of the laughingthrush subfamily, "Garrulacinae". All are also members of the babbler family, "Timaliidae". Several species of laughingthrushes, the Hwamei included, have beautiful and melodious songs. It is for the fine quality of its song that the Hwamei is captured and sold on the caged bird market. The Hwamei, like the Crested Mynah, can imitate the calls of other bird species.

The family, laughingthrush, gets its name from the chattering and laughter-like calls of the members of its less musical members.

China is the center of distribution for all laughingthrushes, and most are found here. Many species of laughingthrushes are found only in Western China. The Hwamei is exclusively an eastern bird in this country. All laughingthrushes are non-migratory, insect and fruit eating birds that generally live at southern latitudes where insects and fruit are readily available all year round.

The Chinese range of the Hwamei extends from the southeast coast of the country including Hainan and Taiwan, northwards through the eastern half of the country to around Shanghai.

The Hwamei is an attractive, if not colorful species of uniformly brown plumage with its distinctive white eye ring from which the bird derives its name.

Despite many individuals being taken out the wild by the caged bird market, the Hwamei remains a fairly common bird throughout its Chinese range.

Hwamei (Photo by Charles Lam)

Japanese Sparrow Hawk (Accipiter gularis)
(27 cm.) Male: small; narrower tail bands than other accipiters; dark grey
upperparts; rufous bars on white underparts; grey tail with several dark bands
Female: Upperparts grey; heavily barred whitish underparts

The Japanese Sparrow Hawk is bird of prey with special adaptations for hunting
and killing prey just like other hawks, owls, eagles, and falcons. This species is a
member of the "accipitridae" subfamily, also known as the "accipiters". Accipiters
are generally smaller than other birds of prey with long tails and short, broad
rounded wings which provide them with exceptional mobility and an acute sense of
sight which is several times better than human sight. All accipiters have sharply
hooked bills.

These birds need their great mobility and sight due to the fact that they are forest
dwelling birds which must navigate around trees when they pursue their favorite
food, other bird species. Their powers of sight, which are even better than other
birds of prey are more acute due to the darker forest environments that they
frequent.

The Japanese Sparrow Hawk is a common member of its family within its Chinese
range. This bird breeds in the extreme northeast of the country and winters in
southeast China and south to Indonesia and the Philippines. It is a common sight
between its summer and winter ranges during summer and fall. During migration it
travels in flocks unlike most other birds of prey which are usually seen migrating
alone.

This species is very small for a bird of prey, and is similar in appearance to other
Chinese accipiters such as the Chinese Sparrow Hawk and the Besra. Its very small
size and very narrow tail bands set it apart from these birds. Females of this species
are larger than males. All accipiters are heavily barred on their wings, bodies and
tails.

The Japanese Sparrow hawk hunts by pursuing smaller birds, usually songbirds, in
flight and capturing them with their superior speed and flying skills. Once caught,
the prey is killed with powerful talons.

Japanese Sparrow Hawk (Photo by Tumi Nagoya)

Japanese White-eye (Zosterops japonicus) Anlu xiuyanniao
(10 cm.) Small; green-olive upperparts; white eye-ring; yellow throat and vent

The Japanese White-eye is the most common of three white-eye species that occur in China. All white-eyes drive their names from, not surprisingly, the white eye rings that each member of the family possesses. They are all small songbirds. There are other small songbirds, however that also possess white eye rings such as several species of flycatcher, so one should not automatically assume that a bird with an eye ring is a member of this family.

The Japanese White-eye, like other members of its family, "Zosteropidae," the white-eyes, is an omnivore that has a wide and varied diet. They will take insects and fruits and even visit flowers to drink the sweet nectar that is available.

This species is extremely active and like many warbler species, it is often difficult to observe due to its hyper-active pace. Fortunately, its white eye ring and yellow body is quite conspicuous, and it is very quickly identifiable.

Of the three white-eye species which occur in China, only two inhabit the east part of the country, the Japanese White-eye and its close cousin, the Chestnut-flanked White-eye. The species look alike both having green backs, yellow throats, and white under parts. However, the Chestnut-flanked White-eye has very obvious brown strips on its side, so separating the two species is not difficult. Sometimes, these two species will flock together.

The Japanese White-eye builds a cup-shaped nest made of a variety of building materials such as hair, spider webs, moss and lichen. It will even steal materials from the nests of other birds.

This bird is admirable for its beauty as well as its role in helping to control insect populations. In 1929, it was introduced to Hawaii in an attempt by authorities there to control insect populations on that ecologically-challenged group of islands.

Japanese White-eye (Photo by Dick Daniels)

Large-billed Crow (Corvus macrorhynchos) Dazui wuya
(50 cm.) Glossy black; long heavy bill; square tail

The Large-billed Crow, often referred to as the "Jungle Crow", is another member of the family, "Corvidae," which includes jays and magpies. It is a typical family member in many ways. Like magpies, jays and other crows, it is an omnivore which can eat just about anything. This species is intelligent, so much so, that it has even been credited with tool using intelligence. It is an aggressive bird that will readily resort to predation as a food gathering technique. As this bird is an omnivore, it could be argued that its predation is unnecessary behavior.

In China, the crow is considered a sign of bad luck. Its close cousin, the Black-billed Magpie, is considered as a sign of good luck and is often called, the "lucky bird". However, it seems that the bad luck tag should be attached to both these birds as they both share some nasty habits. The Large-billed Crow is the perhaps the crow species most likely to attack and kill live domestic chickens. It will also kill other bird species, and other small vertebrates as well.

In addition to prey items that are part of its diet, the Large-billed Crow consumes a wide variety of animal and plant matter, both living and dead. This tremendous versatility in diet has allowed this species to be very adaptable and settle in places, such islands, where they can quickly become a nuisance to local people and wildlife.

As could be expected for such an adaptable bird, the Large-billed Crow is a very widespread species, and is found from eastern China west as far as Iran. Its range in south extends as far as the Philippines. Due to its great versatility in eating habits, it has no need to migrate.

In breeding season, this species builds a platform nest of sticks which is set high in a tree. It seems to prefer fir or pine trees as a nesting site. The female lays 4-5 eggs.

The Large-billed Crow is known for its tendency to form large groups at nighttime roosting sites. At times, especially during the non-breeding season, thousands of these birds can gather at one roosting site the pass the night away surrounded by friendly neighbors.

Large-billed Crow (Photo by JM Garg)

Light-vented Bulbul (Pycnonotus sinensis)
(17 cm.)Olive colored, white throat, white cheek, crest spot

The Light-vented Bulbul which gets its name from its white vent-the area on its body directly under its tail, is one of the commonest birds in Eastern China. In fact, it is sometimes called, "Chinese Bulbul". It is a noisy and gregarious species that form loose flocks for foraging throughout the year. It is quite an attractive species of bulbul and the only member of its family whose range extends north beyond the tropics. As such it is the only bulbul found throughout much of mainland China.

This species is an omnivore which will eat berries and other soft fruits as well as insects. It will often find a high perch in a treetop and wait for flying insects to pass by. It will then leap from its perch and snap up the passing insect in much the same manner as a flycatcher.

The Light-vented Bulbul constructs a cup-shaped nest made primarily from course grasses. It breeds early in the nesting season as it is non-migratory throughout much of its range. The female bulbul usually lays 3-4 eggs.

This species frequents open woodland and cultivated land such as orchards and farms. Like the Black-billed Magpie, the Light-vented Bulbul is well-suited to urban living as city parks and gardens offer the sort of open habitat that this bird favors. It is quite common to find loose flocks of this species in the company of magpies.

The Light-vented Bulbul is thriving throughout its range and its population is strong. As such, one can reasonably expect to see this species in most city parks in China from Hong Kong northwards up the east coast to around Dalian. This is also an extremely common bird throughout much of Korea and Japan.

Light-vented Bulbul (Photo by Charles Lam)

Little Egret (Egretta garzetta)

(60 cm.) Small; long legs, long bill, all white

The Little Egret is a semi-cosmopolitan species of egret that can be found in three continents-Africa, Europe, and Asia. Like the Chinese Pond Heron, it is a member of the family, "Ardeidae", the herons, egrets and bitterns.

In China, the Little Egret is found during the summer breeding season throughout most of central and east China as far north as approximately Dalian, although this species may be pushing its breeding range further north. It is a year –round resident in Taiwan and much of the southern coastline of the country. Sightings of the birds in winter in many parts of its breeding range suggest that it may be pushing its range of year-round residency as well.

The Little Egret is hardly a small bird, its name reflecting the enormous size of some members of its family. It is smaller version of another entirely white egret with black legs and bill, the Great Egret. The Little Egret is a very common bird throughout its Chinese range.

Like all members of its family, the Little Egret hunts for aquatic animals in a wide variety of marine environments. It will consume insects, frogs, fish, crustaceans and reptiles. This bird will hunt in anyplace that has shallow water in which it can wade in search of food. Sometimes, this bird is seen standing completely still watching the water's surface and waiting for its prey to appear. Other times, it can be seen moving the water with its feet in an attempt to disturb motionless fish.

The Little Egret is another colony breeder which will share its colony with other species of wading birds. The female lays 3-5 eggs on a platform nest of sticks in a tree or bush. Both male and female Little Egrets attend to the incubation of eggs and the subsequent caring for chicks.

The Little Egret, and other egret species were once hunted to near extinction in some parts of world during the 19th century. They were killed for the long feathers that adorn the heads of the males during breeding season. These feathers became popular fashion accessories on women's hats during that era. After egret populations had fallen to dangerously low levels, many conservation efforts were initiated and the birds rebounded.

Little Egret (Photo by JM Garg)

Little Grebe (Tachybaptus ruficollis) Xiao piti

(27 cm.) Breeding:small; dark; throat and neck reddish; crown and back of neck grayish brown; upperparts brown; underparts grey Non-breeding: upperparts grayish-brown; underparts white; black bill

The Little Grebe, also known as "Dabchick," is a small and common member of the duck-like family, "Podicipedidae," the family of grebes. This bird has a semi-cosmopolitan distribution and can be found in most parts of the world excluding the Americas and Australia. It can be found all over eastern and central China where it is all season resident except in the far north. Individuals which breed in "Dongbei" migrate to warmer parts of the country in fall.

All grebes are duck-like water birds which feed by diving in their aquatic lake and ocean habitats. They differ from ducks in their more pointed bills, shorter wings, more erect necks, and lobed, rather than webbed feet.

The Little Grebe is found in summer in the lakes, and wetlands which offer plenty of open water and water vegetation. They can even be found breeding in city parks in many eastern cities in the country.

The Little Grebe is an excellent hunter of fish and other aquatic animal species. It can remain underwater for several minutes during its dives in search of prey. It is also an excellent swimmer with its specially adapted lobed toes which nature designed for speed in water. It uses aquatic vegetation to conceal itself when on its hunting missions.

As a bird which is so dependant on water, the Little Grebe nests at the water's edge. Grebes, due to their adaptations for swimming, have trouble moving on land. Their legs are set far to their posterior, making walking on land difficult. The female Little Grebe usually lays 4-7 eggs on a nest made of floating vegetation. When the mother grebe leaves her eggs to venture out on her fishing tasks, she covers her eggs with weeds to conceal them from predators.

In the breeding season prior to mating, Little Grebes engage in animated courtship displays which sees the birds running over the water's surface and uttering their high-pitched calls, "ke-ke-ke-ke!

Little Grebe (Andreas Trepte, www.photo-natur.de)

Little Ringed Plover (Charadrius dubius) Heiling xing
(16 cm.) Small; small bill; single thick dark band across chest; yellow legs; conspicuous yellow eye-ring; no wing bars

The Little Ringed Plover is part of a very large family subfamily of small wading birds with straight bills which are notched at the tip, the plovers. The plover family is known according to scientific classification as the "Charadriinae" family. Plovers are found feeding for small invertebrates at the water edge's and open land.

This species is one of the smallest of its family. Like many plovers, it has a black mask and a ring around its neck. The Common Ringed Plover looks very similar but the Little Ringed Plover's completely black bill, thinner neck ring, and conspicuous eye-ring distinguish it from this bird.

The Little Ringed Plover is a widespread species that is found in North Africa in winter and most of Europe and Asia throughout the year. In China, this species breeds throughout the eastern and central parts of the country. It winters in the southeast of China and Southeast Asia.

The diet of this species consists mostly of worms and insects of various species.

This species is usually found in marshes, mudflats, and along the sandy banks of rivers and streams.

This is a widespread and common species in eastern China, and it is likely to be encountered by anyone who watches out for it.

Little Ringed Plover (Photo by Marek Szczpanek)

Long-tailed Tit (Aegithalos caudatus) Yinhou shanque
(16 cm.) Small black bill; tiny body; very long tail with white edges; different races vary in color pattern

The Long-tailed Tit, due to its elongated tail and more conical bill is place in a separate family, "Aegithalidae", from other most other tit species such as the Great Tit. The members of the Long-tailed Tits family are all tits which share the characteristic of the long tail.

The Long-tailed Tit is a common bird in Europe and Asia and several races exist that vary in appearance. All races of these races are easily recognizable as members of this species, however. In China, this bird is a non-migratory resident species that lives only in the eastern half of the country from Heilongjiang in the north to around Shanghai in the south.

All tits species regardless of which family they are placed in are very active and acrobatic birds which can usually be found amid the boughs of trees foraging for insects and seeds. Tits are generally non-migratory birds due to their omnivorous diet and their ability to switch to a strictly vegetarian in winter if needed. As a result, tits, and their North American cousins, the chickadees, are birds often found in far northern latitudes in wintertime. Birdwatchers are grateful that these cheerful and usually quite tame little creatures are present during the cold winter months.

Unlike most tits, the Long-tailed Tit is primarily an insect eater throughout the year.

This bird favors deciduous or mixed woodlands as its habitat. In winter, it prefers deciduous forests that can still yield insects.

Due to the small size of its body, this bird is susceptible to extreme cold in wintertime. During extremely cold spells, the majority of the Long-tailed Tit population in a particular place can perish. However, the remaining birds are able to breed prodigiously to replace the loss.

Long-tailed Tit (Photo by Francis C. Franklin)

Mallard (Anas platyrhynchos)
(58 cm.) Male: yellow bill; green head; brown chest; white neck-ring; grey underparts. Female: mottled brown upperparts and underparts; orange bill and legs.

The Mallard is one of the most well known birds in the world. It is found across the Northern Hemisphere and in Australia and New Zealand. It is a member of the avian family, "Anatidae", which includes ducks, geese, and swans. It is also often referred to as a "dabbling" duck due to its method of finding food while in water.

Ducks are often placed in two categories, "diving" ducks and "dabbling" ducks.

Diving ducks are those ducks which will, while in water, dive beneath the surface, often to great depths, to capture food. These ducks are usually seafaring species such as scaup and scoters. Dabbling ducks, often also referred to as "pond" ducks for their love of freshwater, do not dive but instead turn their heads and bodies into the water with the posterior of the bird still seen above water. Diving ducks are generally fish eating species which must dive to chase their prey, while dabbling ducks tend to be vegetarians or omnivores which don't need to pursue prey.

The male Mallard is instantly recognizable with its trademark green head, yellow bill, and white neck ring. Even many people who are not particularity interested in birds can identify a male Mallard. The female, like females of many bird species, is a drab brown creature.

In China, Mallards breed in the extreme northeast of the country and in some locations in the west. They are a year-round resident in most of the east and central regions of the country. They are extremely adaptable and can inhabit a wide range of habitats including both salt and freshwater environments.

This species is an omnivore which shows a fondness for animal and plant matter equally. Insects, snails, worms, and a wide variety of plant species constitute its diet. In. winter, when small invertebrates are not available, plants constitute the majority of it diet.

During breeding season the female Mallard will lay a large clutch of eggs, usually 10-12, in a nest which the female tries to locate far from predators. Often a Mallard nest will contain eggs from other duck species. Females of other species sometimes try to get the Mallard female to raise their chicks. If the female Mallard notices that some eggs were not laid by her, she will usually neglect them.

Mallard (Photo by Anton Holmquist)

Mandarin Duck (Atix galericulata) Yuanyang
(40cm.) Male: unmistakable Female: brownish-grey plumage; white eye-ring/eye-line.

The Mandarin Duck is a bird of such extraordinary beauty that it must be considered as one of the most beautiful animals in the world. The male of the species is so elaborately adorned that a text description will fail to do the bird justice. Needless to say, this bird is absolutely gorgeous and unmistakable and needs no further words. The female, although a much less elaborate creature than the male, is also attractive. The Mandarin Duck is included in the large family of ducks, geese and swans, "Anatidae".

Unfortunately, this extremely attractive bird is now one the rarest wild birds in China. Once quite common and widespread in Asia, the Mandarin Duck's population declined drastically due to the destruction of its forest habitat and capture and export as a decorative species.

Today, the bird is found in the wild in Russia, China and Japan. Fewer than 1000 pairs of Mandarin Ducks can be found in China in the wild. A similar number can be found in Russia, while Japan is still home to 5000 pairs of wild Mandarin Ducks. Many specimens are kept in zoos around the world, and these are the only places that most people today can hope to see this special bird.

The few remaining wild Mandarin Ducks in China today breed in the forests of the extreme northeast of the country. In fall and spring they migrate along the East Coast to their wintering grounds in the south.

Fortunately, Mandarin Ducks introduced to the wild in other parts of the world have build up significant populations. A reported 7000 pairs of the birds can be found in Britain. Berlin, Germany also has a large local population of the birds. In America, Mandarin Ducks which escaped from captivity have established a population of several hundred in Sonoma County, California.

In the wild, Mandarin Ducks nest in tree cavities near lakes and ponds. They eat plants, seeds, fish, snails, and insects. They feed by dabbling in the manner of the Mallard.

This bird has been immortalized in Chinese art for centuries as a symbol of marital bliss and fidelity.

Mandarin Duck (Photo by Arpingstone)

Orange-flanked Bush Robin (Tarsiger cyanurus)
(13 cm.) Male: blue upperparts; orange flanks; white underparts; white eye-line.
Female: uniformly grey-brown upperparts; orange flanks; blue tail; white throat and
underparts.

The Orange-flanked Bush Robin is a small, brightly colored and delightfully tame
species of songbird that is a common sight among the bushes of city parks and
gardens. It is a delight to encounter due to its usually friendly disposition, allowing
humans to approach within close range before flying off.

This species gets in name from the orange stripes along its sides, or "flanks". The
male of the species is very beautiful with a deep blue back and tail, orange flanks,
and white under parts. The female of the species is grayish-brown with a blue tail
and the diagnostic orange flanks. This stark difference in coloration between males
and females is typical of its family.

It is a member of the family, "Mucacipidae", with other robins and flycatchers. Like
al members of this family, this species is an insectivore, or insect eater. This bird

will usually be found low in bushes or on the ground in search of its favorite food.

This is another very widespread species that breeds as throughout much of East Asia as far west as Finland and reaching Japan in its easternmost range. In China, its breeding range is limited to Heilongjiang and Jilin provinces. In the breeding season, this bird is found nesting in mixed coniferous forests. The nest is usually on or near the ground and will contain 3-5 eggs which are incubated by the female only.

With the completion of its breeding, the Orange-flanked Bush Robin will begin its long trek to its southern wintering grounds in south and central China and Southeast Asia. In winter, this bird can be found as far north as Shanghai.

Orange-flanked Bush Robin (Photo by JM Garg)

Oriental Grey-capped Greenfinch (Carduelis sinica)
Grey, yellow, and brown; thick pink bill, yellow patch on wing (13 cm.)

In the Northeastern United States and Canada, birdwatchers have a special term for a group of birds that are usually only seen in winter, "winter finches". These are members of the finch family that breed far north near the Arctic Circle. IN winter, they venture south where they are seen by birdwatchers.

For those of us living in Northern China, the Grey-capped Greenfinch (also called Chinese Greenfinch) is one of those birds. It is a finch, and it is normally only seen in the mainland come winter.

Like all finches and especially those that live in cold climates during winter, the Grey-capped Greenfinch is primarily a seed-eater. This species favors cultivated places such as farmland and other similar open country for living. They will often be found in winter on the edges of coniferous forests where they search various types of coniferous trees for seed-bearing cones. This species will also take various types of insects during the summer breeding season.

Oriental Grey-capped Greenfinch (Photo by Alpsdake)

Oriental Magpie Robin (Copsychus saularis) Que qu
(20 cm.) Male: Black head, throat and breast; white underparts; black and white wings and tail. Female: Like male except for grey head and breast.

The Oriental Magpie Robin, which is a common sight in south China parks, is an unmistakable bird which looks like a much smaller version of the Black-billed Magpie. Once placed in the family of thrushes, "Turdidae," it is now considered a species in the family, "Muscicapidae," the family of flycatchers.

This species is a non-migratory bird of Bangladesh, India, Pakistan, and southeast Asia, including China, Indonesia, Thailand and the Philippines. In this country, it is found in the southern half of the country. It is also found in the central portion of the country, as well as Tibet.

The male of the species is a beautifully patterned black and white bird, while the female is a greyer version of the male.

The Oriental Magpie Robin favors open wooded areas and cultivated areas such as gardens and parks. This preference of habitat makes it an ideal city-dweller.

During the breeding season, the male if the species becomes extremely animated often singing loudly from a perch high in a tree while puffing his feathers and fanning his tail in his attempts to attract a mate. After mating, the female will lay 4-5 eggs in a nest constructed by her in a cavity of a tree or wall. The female takes most of the responsibility for the raising of chicks. The male will aggressively defend their nesting territory during this time.

This bird is primarily an insectivore with its diet consisting mainly of insects and other invertebrates. On occasion, they will consume small lizards and even fish.

The Oriental Magpie Robin is still a fairly common bird within its Chinese range, but its population has declined, especially around Hong Kong, due to frequent capture for the caged bird trade and the introduction of invasive species such as the Common Mynah.

As a bird of such striking beauty, this species is well-loved throughout its Asian range. It is highly admired by cage bird collectors for its beautiful singing, and it is the national bird of Bangladesh.

Oriental Magpie Robin (Photo by JM Garg)

Oriental Reed Warbler (Acrocephalus sophiae)
(19 cm.) large warbler, brownish above, white below, whitish stripe over eye, throat streaks

The Oriental Reed Warbler is one of the biggest species of warbler in China. Its large size is typical of its ilk. It is a member of the family, Acrocephalidae, also known as the "marsh warblers." The marsh warblers are so named due to their love of marshy habitat. They are generally much larger than other warbler species and are brownish birds without streaks or wing bars. All have whitish under parts.

The Oriental Reed Warbler is a bird of eastern Asia, and it breeds throughout the eastern half of China except the extreme southern part along the coast including

Hong Kong and Taiwan. It will be seen in these places during its migrations to and from its wintering grounds in Southeast Asia.

Like all warbler species, this bird is an insectivore that eats insects and other small invertebrates and only occasionally peppers its diet with other food substances. As an insectivore that breeds in northern latitudes, it must migrate each winter to warmer climates where active insects can be found.

In addition to marshes, this bird can be found in rice fields and brushy areas

During the breeding season, the male Oriental Reed Warbler will sing from an exposed perch such as the tip of a reed stem or bush. His song is a mixture of warbling notes and less musical guttural ones. The territories established by singing male birds are small and a colony of densely concentrated pairs of Oriental Reed Warblers can be found in a single marsh.

The female lays 2-6 eggs in the nest which is situated among reed stems. Often, the Common Cuckoo, a "brood parasite" will lay an egg in the nest of the reed warblers. Besides this intrusion, mother reed warblers must also be wary of predators such as weasels and snakes.

Oriental Reed Warbler (Photo by JM Garg)

Oriental Turtle Dove (Streptopelia orientalis) Shan banjiu
(32 cm.) Pinkish plumage; whitish striped patch on neck; dark scalloped plumage on upperparts; grey rump

The Oriental Turtle Dove, also known as the Rufous Turtle Dove, is a member of the family, "Columbiformes," which includes doves and pigeons. This is another dove species which has a prominent neck patch. The Spotted Dove has a conspicuous patch of spots on its neck while the Oriental Turtle Dove has a patch of stripes. The Oriental Turtle Dove is a slightly larger version of its European counterpart, the Turtle Dove.

This beautiful bird is a common and widespread species throughout eastern China. It is a resident bird in most of its range which encompasses the eastern half of China and parts of the west. Birds which breed in the Northern provinces will migrate south to find somewhat warmer climates. Some birds will migrate as far south as

Much like the other common dove species in eastern China, the Spotted Dove, this species is a gentle creature that subsists on almost entirely plant matter. Seeds, and various fruits and berries constitute the majority of its diet. This bird acquires its food by foraging on the ground. The similarities between the Spotted Dove and the Oriental Turtle Dove are reflected in the inclusion of both species within the genus, "Streptopelia."

The Oriental Turtle Dove is usually found in the company of its mate while engaging peacefully in its food gathering. This bird frequents open agricultural areas and small villages.

All dove and pigeon species share very similar nesting choices and brood sizes. All build loose, rather flimsy-looking platform nests set in trees into which female birds deposit two white eggs.

Oriental Turtle Dove (Photo by Ravi Vaidyanathan)

Osprey (Pandion haliaetus) Yu'e
(55 cm.) Dark brown neck, back, wings, and tail; white throat, crown and

underparts; dark mask.

The Osprey is a truly cosmopolitan species of raptor which can be found on every continent on earth except Antarctica. It is also called Fish Hawk or Fish Eagle due to its heavy reliance on fish as a component of its diet. It is the sole member of its subfamily, "Pandioninae". The fact that the Osprey is the single member of its family living world-wide makes it a unique bird.

The Osprey, which looks like a small eagle, is the sole member of its family due several physical differences between it and other diurnal birds of prey. Unlike eagles and hawks, the Osprey has a reversible toe which enables it to place two talons pointing backwards on its foot. Also, its toes are of equal length, and its talons are rounded as opposed to grooved. Furthermore, the Osprey's feet are equipped with sharp barbs that make grasping fish an easier task. These differences in feet are specific adaptations to its fish-hunting way of life.

In China, the Osprey is found over much of the eastern and western parts of the country, but it is absent from much of the central region. In eastern China, it is a resident species in Dongbei and the south coast from around Xiamen to Hong Kong. It is also a resident species of Taiwan.

The Osprey is an unmistakable bird due to its distinctive dark brown mask, wings, body and tail, and otherwise white plumage. Males and females look alike, although males can be identified by their slimmer bodies and narrower wings.

The Osprey is well-named Fish Eagle as fish constitute around 99% of its diet. The other one per cent is made up of the occasional rodent, rabbit, reptile, or other birds. Ospreys catch fish by hovering over the water's surface until a fish is sighted and then diving feet first into the water. At other times, the Osprey can avoid diving by swooping over the water's surface and snatching fish from just below the surface. Closeable nostrils prevent water from entering the bird during its fishing activities.

Osprey nests are platforms of sticks which can be found in trees, on utility poles, or even on large rocks. The female lays 2-4 eggs, and incubates them for around 5 weeks. Young Ospreys take several months to gain full independence from their parents. Ospreys generally mate for life.

Osprey (Photo by Mike Baird)

Pacific Swift (Apus pacificus) Biaoyao yuyan

(18 cm.) Large for swift; long, deeply-forked tail; dark brown plumage; white rump; white chin.

The Pacific Swift, which was formerly known as the Fork-Tailed Swift is one of a family of very fast-flying, insectivorous birds, the swifts, of the family, "Apodidae." All swifts get their names from the speed of their flight, "swift" is a synonym of "fast", in English. All swifts are small birds that look similar to swallows; however, they are more closely related to hummingbirds.

Swifts have long, backwards pointing wings and either very long or short tails. They all have very small legs as they are birds of the sky that rarely perch in trees or on wires. They spend most of their waking hours in flight and will rest by gripping the sides of cliffs, buildings, or any vertical surface with their sharp claws. Swifts have small bills, but the gape of their mouths is very large, an adaptation that allows them to easily trap flying insects when they are in flight.

Most swifts are difficult to identify, but this one is easily distinguished by its larger size, white chin, white rump patch, and dusky-brown plumage.

Pacific Swifts are found from central Siberia eastwards through Asia. In China, they breed in the northeast portion of the country from the Shanghai area northward up to Heilongjiang. South of Shanghai, all the way down to Hong Kong, they are resident birds that do not migrate.

Pacific Swifts build their nests on cliffs, and the female lays 2-3 eggs in the nest. After hatching, both parents will hunt insects to feed their hungry chicks, often traveling great distances in their searches for food. Pacific Swifts will return to their nests year after year, rebuilding or repairing them when necessary.

This species is usually seen in flocks, flying over open areas. They will often mix with mixed flocks of other swift species. The aerial antics of this bird is truly impressive when it is in the midst of its insect-hunting missions. No other bird was ever better equipped for life in the sky.

(Photo by Osma)

Red-billed Leiothrix (Leiothrix lutea) Hongzui xiangsiniao
(15 cm.) Red bill; thick white eye-ring; orange breast; yellow belly; yellow patches
on wings

The Red-billed Leiothrix is a colorful species of the babbler family, "Timaliidae."
Despite the fact that the bird is fairly common, it is rarely seen. This is due to its
love of dense jungle and pine forest habitats with dense ground vegetation that
allows the bird to remain hidden from most observers. This species is often called
by other names such as Pekin Robin, Pekin Nightingale and Japanese Nightingale
despite not being native to Japan.

All babblers, this species included, share certain common traits which help to
distinguish them from other songbirds. Babblers are usually quite gregarious, liking
the company others of their kind. Most have harsh, chattering and unmusical calls
unlike the more pleasing sounds of other songbird species. Most babblers tend to be
"sedentary" or inactive, and remain close to the ground. They are poor fliers and as
such do not undertake migrations.

The Red-billed Leiothrix is an omnivore which eats both plant and animal matter. It
feeds among the vegetation on or close to the ground of its forest and jungle

habitats. It is fond of fruits such as strawberries, guava and papaya and many types of insects.

In the summer breeding season, this species makes an open cup-shaped nest of a type similar to other babblers which is usually situated close to the ground in a shrub. The nest is usually composed of leaves, moss and lichen. As the nest is placed in a shrub surrounded by other dense vegetation, it is usually well hidden from predators. The female lays 2-4 eggs with 3 eggs being the normal clutch size.

In China, the Red-billed Leiothrix is found throughout the southeastern mainland from the South Coast as far north as approximately the Shanghai region.

The Red-billed Leiothrix and the Hwamei are two Chinese songbird species which have been introduced widely to other locations around the world. Both species have been introduced in Hawaii and thrived. In other places such as Australia, France and England, the Red-billed Leiothrix was introduced but failed to remain. Hawaii is much richer today for the presence of this lovely Chinese bird.

Red-billed Leiothrix (Photo by Dick Daniels)

Russet Sparrow (Passer rutilans) Shan maque
(14-15 cm.) Male: Bright cinnamon crown and upperparts; black streaks on back; black throat; whitish cheeks. Female: dark brown upperparts; two conspicuous eye-stripes-one white, one dark

The Russet Sparrow is a chunky bird which looks much like any typical sparrow. In fact, its markings are very much like its close cousin, the much more ubiquitous, Eurasian House Sparrow. However, the male of this species bears plumage which is a shade of brown not often seen in sparrows, bright cinnamon. The striking bright cinnamon of the male Russet Sparrow's back is a diagnostic marking that makes for quick identification in the field. Accordingly, the Russet Sparrow is often called the Cinnamon Sparrow or Cinnamon Tree Sparrow. Like all sparrows, this species is a member of the family, "Passeridae."

As with many songbirds, this species exhibits "sexual dimorphism" in its plumage, as the males look much different than the females. In the case of songbirds, this means that the males are far more colorful and attractive than the females.

The Chinese range of the Russet Sparrow comprises most of its world-wide range. It is found in the eastern half of China from Hong Kong and Taiwan as far north as the Shandong peninsula, and in Korea and Japan in the east and northern India in the west. Throughout most of its Chinese range, the Russet Sparrow is a resident bird. It is a summer breeding visitor in the northern parts of its Chinese range.

The Russet Sparrow is a bird of open woodland and scrub near cultivation. In places where Eurasian Tree Sparrows are scarce, the Russet Sparrow can fulfill that bird's role as a denizen of cities and villages.

The Russet Sparrow's diet consists of mostly seeds which it collects while foraging on the ground like the Eurasian Tree Sparrow. In agricultural areas, this species can become a pest as it will damage grain crops through feeding; however, it will also so kill and collect many insect pests that damage crops to feed to its growing chicks.

During the breeding season, the male Russet Sparrow will choose a nesting site from which he will perform his courtship display. He will bob his head and puff his chest at passing females and eventually bow to a prospective mate in true Asian style. When a female accepts his advances, the pair of birds will build a nest in a tree cavity, usually the abandoned nest of a woodpecker. The female will lay 5-6 glossy-white eggs.   In the northern parts of their breeding range, Russet Sparrows show a fondness for high altitudes as nesting sites.

Russet Sparrow (Photo by JM Garg)

Spotted Dove (Streptopelia Chinensis)
Pinkish brown long tail, black spotted patch on side of neck, white on the tip of the tail; large (30 cm.)

The Spotted Dove, named for the speckled patch on its neck, is a pigeon, often generically referred to in Chinese as "Ge Zi". It should be noted that there is more than one type of pigeon, and that the Spotted Dove is an entirely wild variety of pigeon and should not be confused with domestic pigeons which are raised by man. As its scientific name, "Streptopelia chinesis," suggests, it is also known as the "Chinese Dove."

Although it is closely related to domestic pigeons, one who encounters it in the field will quickly notice a difference in its temperament. Unlike the domestic pigeons that inhabit the cities in eastern China, this species is not approachable. In keeping with its completely wild status, this bird will not allow humans to venture too close.

It is very shy, indeed. Even in city parks where people are common, the Spotted Dove has not lost its in-born fear of humans.

The Spotted Dove is a member of the order, "Columbiformes", which contains all species of doves. The Spotted Dove, admired for its beauty and demure personality has been successfully introduced to many locations outside Asia including Australia, New Zealand, Hawaii, and even southern California.

The Spotted Dove, in keeping with its gentle nature is entirely an herbivore, feeding on vegetation, seeds and grain which it finds during its foraging sessions on the ground. It is a bird of open woodland, farms, and parks, making it well suited to life in and outside the city. It is not a social species, and will usually be found alone or with its mate.

The Spotted Dove, like other members of its order, mates for life, showing true devotion to its mate. As a non-migratory species, this species breeds early in the spring with the female dove depositing two shiny white eggs in a nest. Both the male and female parents attend to the feeding of chicks and both parents can produce "pigeon milk" in their crops to help sustain the growing chicks.

The dove is the international symbol of peace, and the beautiful Spotted Dove conducts its business in a manner befitting this image.

Spotted Dove (Photo by Dick Daniels)

Tristram's Bunting (Embiriza tristrami)
(15 cm.) Male: Bold black face pattern; white eye-line and mustache'; white spot behind ear; brown breast; white belly. Female: duller version of male's face pattern; brown eye-line and mustache'; yellow spot behind ear.

Tristram's Bunting is just one of several species of bunting that can be found in East China. All buntings are members of the large finch family which includes various birds called "finch," sparrows, buntings, and grosbeaks.

All of these birds have thick, powerful conical bills which they use to crack open nuts and seeds. Buntings are similar in size to sparrows, although most buntings in China possess some colors besides brown, most often yellow. The females of most bunting species closely resemble sparrows and each other as they are generally brown with markings very similar to sparrows and females of other bunting species.

The male and female Tristram's Bunting is a somewhat more distinctive species due to the unique black and white face pattern of the male which is seen in more muted tones on the face of the female.

The summer breeding range, fall and spring migration range and wintering range constitutes almost exactly the whole eastern portion of China. There is very little of this birds' range that falls outside the Chinese mainland.

In the north China in the summer, Tristram's Buntings nest in the thick forests found in this part of the country. During its spring and fall, this species is a common sight in city parks and gardens where it can be found on the ground searching for food.

In winter, this bird can be found along the South Coast from around Xiamen to Hong Kong and few hundred kilometers inland along this stretch of coastline.

Tristram's Bunting (Photo by Alder Chang)

Tufted Duck (Aythya fuligula)
(42 cm.) Male: black head, chest, back, and tail; white sides and underparts; narrow tuft extending from back of head. Female: uniformly brown with head tuft.

The Tufted Duck is small, fast flying duck species that is a member of the duck subfamily, "Aythyinae." Members of this family are all "diving ducks" which dive deep under water to pursue fish and other aquatic animals. This male of this species is entirely black except for its white flanks and blue-grey bill. The female is brown with paler flanks.

The bird's name is derived from a conspicuous crest, or "tuft" which extends from the back of its head.

This species is found throughout the temperate regions of Europe and Asia. In winter, it is an occasional visitor to North America. In China, it is a common species which can be found in the northeast in summer and the southeast in winter. During its migrations in spring and fall, it can be found en route between these locations.

The Tufted Duck is a freshwater diving duck which can be found in the breeding season in freshwater lakes and ponds which are located close to marshes that provide tall vegetation in which the female can conceal her nest. It is believed that the range of the Tufted Duck is expanded due to the expansion of the range of freshwater mussels, one of its favorite foods.

In addition to mussels, the Tufted Duck will eat other mollusks and aquatic insects.

Tufted Duck (Photo by Dick Daniels)

Vinous-throated Parrotbill (Paradoxornis webbianis)
(12 cm.) small; long tail; small parrot-like bill; uniformly brown with light streaks on throat.

The Vinous-throated Parrotbill is an interesting and rather unconventional species of songbird of the former parrotbill family, "Paradoxornithidae." The latin name of the this family translates to English as "paradox bird," meaning a bird that cannot be understood. For many years ornithologists had struggled to find the correct classification for the parrotbills. Originally, they had been placed in the family, "Paridae," the family of tits with which they do share some habits. However, after strict observations of DNA, they were moved to Paradoxornithidae, and finally, "Sylviidae, the family of warblers.

The species gets its name from its hooked bill which resembles that of very small parrot. Several species of parrotbills can be found in China, but most are tropical species only found in the extreme south of the country, This species is found almost throughout the eastern half of the country only missing in western parts of Jilin and Heilongjiang. No other parrotbill can be found at these latitudes.

This species is one of the smallest of the family, and it has a proportionally much longer tail than other parrotbills. Its plumage is uniformly brown, and it derives its name from the faint brown streaks found on its throat. Males and females look alike.

The Vinous-throated Parrotbill is a an extremely gregarious species that is usually found in large loose flocks of birds which are at their biggest during the winter. In winter, flocks can exceed 100 individuals. In summer, when breeding is occupying the mated pairs of birds, these flocks are much smaller.

This bird is extremely adaptable and hardy. It can survive in a wide range of habitats, including various types of forest, swampland and cultivated places such as farms, orchards and city parks. It is this adaptability that enables the Vinous-throated Parrotbill to live in northern latitudes to harsh for other parrotbills.

The Vinous-throated Parrotbill is always cooperative species to observe as it allows human visitors to approach rather closely as it gleans the branches of trees and bushes in search of its favorite food, seeds.

Vinous-throated Parrotbill (Photo by Alder Chang)

Watercock (Gallicrex   cinera) Dong ji
(40 cm.) Male: large; black   plumage; red frontal plate Female: brown with narrow bars on underparts

Although often very common, rails, like the Watercock, are seldom seen as they frequent habitats that are rarely visited by the average person. Even birdwatchers who seek out these birds in their swampy habitats have a tough time glimpsing one. Most members of the rail family, "Rallidae," are shy, skulking creatures that avoid any human contact if possible. Gallinules and coots are exceptions as they will often be seen swimming in open water in plain view.

The Watercock is one of the shy rails, and its often nocturnal way of life further complicates the chances of ever seeing one. Also, unlike many other bird species that will fly away when surprised by a passing human, rails will instead quietly run into dense vegetation never revealing their presence. On occasion, this bird will venture into rice fields to feed, and it is at these times that a few fortunate people may see it.

The Watercock is found throughout most of Asia from India and Pakistan in the west to Japan in the east, and south as far as Indonesia. Throughout most of its range, it is a non-migratory, resident bird; however, in China it is a summer breeding season visitor, which can be found in the eastern half of the country from Sichuan along the south coast to Hainan and Taiwan and as far north as Liaoning Province.

This bird breeds in the swamps throughout its range where it can find ample tall vegetation in which to hide while it forages for food. It feeds by probing mud and shallow water for insects and small fish. It will also forage on the ground in search of grain and seeds at other times. The body of the Watercock is laterally flattened to allow it to pass easily among the reeds of its swampy home.

The female Watercock will choose a dry patch of ground among swamp vegetation to lay her eggs. A typical clutch is 3-6 eggs. Watercock chicks are entirely black, as with all other rail species.

Although Watercock sightings are rare and difficult to achieve, hearing these birds is not a difficult task at all. This bird is extremely noisy, especially during the summer breeding season when its deep, booming calls can be heard emanating from its swampy domain.

Watercock (Photo by Koshy Koshy)

White Wagtail (Motacilla Alba)
(20 cm.)Wags tail, patchy white and black plumage

The White Wagtail is a less colorful, but more often seen cousin of the Grey Wagtail. Like that species, the While Wagtail is a member of the wagtail family, "moticillidae." The White Wagtail is a "pied" species, meaning that its plumage is made up of just white and black colors. It is a handsomely patterned species, however.

Like its cousin, the Grey Wagtail, the White Wagtail prefers the wet environments of rivers and streams, but it is very versatile and will also be found near farms, gardens and open fields.

This is a widespread species that can be found in Africa, Europe and Asia. In China, the White Wagtail can be found everywhere except for a small patch in the west part of the country. In breeding season this species can be found throughout the northern half of China. It is a resident species as far north as Shandong Province and throughout the southern half of the country.

The White Wagtail is much hardier than other wagtail species, and it can be found far farther north in winter than other members of its family.

White Wagtail (Andreas Trepte, www.photo-natur.de)

White-cheeked Starling (Sturnus cineraceus)
(24 cm.) White cheek on black head; white rump; grey back; orange bill and legs.

Often animal species fulfill ecological needs within their given range. They perform a task that is required to sustain the delicate balance of nature between food producers/consumers and predators/prey. Birds such as starlings are active insect consumers which help to control the population the insects they consume. In west China a species of starling, the Common Starling performs the task of controlling the insect population in open habitats such as fields and farmland. In east China, this task is taken over by another member of the family, the White-cheeked Starling.

The White-cheeked Starling is named for the white spot on the side of its face, or "cheek". Males and females are similar in appearance with the females of the species being of duller coloration.

The breeding range of this species includes northeast China, Korea and Japan and parts of Siberia. In wild areas, it is an adaptable bird which can live in woodland and open country. Its adaptable nature makes it an ideal city-dweller where it can find parks and gardens. It is often seen in city parks along the East Coast of China in the company of Yellow-billed Grosbeaks with which it forms loose feeding flocks in winter.

This species is an omnivore like other starlings. It eats a wide variety of plant and animal matter, but it is especially fond of fruit and crickets.

Like other starling species, this bird is a hole nester which builds a nest in a cavity in a tree. Often it can use holes that once served as nesting places for woodpeckers that have since been abandoned.

A noisy and gregarious bird, the White-cheeked Starling's conspicuous behavior has garnered it attention from birdwatchers and others. The pop culture sensation, Pokemon features a character called, "Starly" which is based entirely on this species.

White-cheeked Starling (Photo by Alpsdake)

White-rumped Munia (Lonchura striata) Baiyao wenniao
(11 cm.) small; brown body; black wings and tail; white rump; white belly

The White-rumped Munia, or as it is often called, the White-rumped Mannikin, despite looking very much like a sparrow, is not a sparrow or even a finch. Instead, it is a member of the family, "Estrildidae," closely related, finch-like birds which are typically found in tropical latitudes as opposed to the more northerly latitudes frequented by true finches. The bill and coloration of the White-rumped Munia gives it a very sparrow-like appearance; however, it should be noted that the bills of all munias, while thick, are longer and more pointed than that of a sparrow.

The White-rumped Munia, although a member of a tropical family, can be found quite far into temperate regions of the country, with Shanghai representing the northern limit of this species Chinese range.

This species is common throughout its range, and can be found in open woodlands, grasslands, city parks and gardens, and other cultivated places.

It is a noisy, gregarious species that can be found in mixed flocks with other munias and birds of other species. It combs the vegetation close to the ground for is food which consists of mainly seeds and at other times, algae which they glean for protein from various water sources.

The nest of this bird is like the nests of other munias, a large, domed structure which is found in a tree, bush or tall grass. The female bird deposits 3-8 eggs into this nest. The White-rumped Munia and other members of the Estrildidae family are often referred to as "weaver-finches" based on their nest-building talents.

Despite the fact that this species is quite common, many people will miss seeing it because it is often hidden in dense vegetation.

White-rumped Munia, (Photo by Vengolis)

Winter Wren (Troglodytes troglodytes) Jiaoliao
(10 cm.) Tiny; tail held erect; faint eye-line; uniformly brown; dark bars on belly.

The Winter Wren is a tiny nomad of a bird. It is the only member of its family, "Troglodytinae," to be found outside of the Americas. This bird, also called the Eurasian Wren, is often simply referred to as "the wren" because it is the only species of its kind in Eurasia. It was also the first species of its family known to science, and to be given the name, "wren." Fifty-nine other species of wren can be found throughout the Americas from Canada down to Argentina.

The family's name, Troglodytinae, means cave-dweller, a reference to all wrens' habit of disappearing into dense vegetation near the ground. All wrens are various shades of brown and all of them hold their tails in an erect, upright position. They are all insectivores that have often beautiful and complex songs.

The Winter Wren is one of the smallest birds within its range throughout the Northern Hemisphere. Its tiny size is one of the keys to its identification, especially in Europe and Asia where it is the only tiny brown bird that cocks its stubby tail in the typical wren-fashion.

In China, the Winter Wren breeds in its year-round range in the northeast and northwest corners of the country. It is also a resident of the central portion of the country and Taiwan. In winter, it can found along the East Coast of the country from Dalian all the way down the coast to Hong Kong.

The Winter Wren has one of the most amazing songs in the bird world. It is also one of the loudest songs for a bird so tiny. The song consists of rising and falling melodious notes and trills of very clear tone, and lasts for up to half a minute. Following another half-minute's rest, the song starts again. Once heard, the song of this bird is never forgotten. The song of this bird, although most often heard in spring can be heard year-round.

The Winter Wren prefers coniferous forests as habitat, and in the summer breeding season, the male builds several round nests of grass, leaves, or moss, allowing the female to choose her favorite. Winter Wrens are polygamous, and a male wren may have several families during one breeding season.

The Winter Wren feeds on spiders and insects, including many that hide in crevices during winter months. This bird's ability to find insect life in the depths of winter allows it to be a non-migratory bird throughout much of its range.

Winter Wren (Photo by Ron Knight)

Yellow-billed Grosbeak (Eophona migratoria)
Large, very thick yellow bill, black wings and head, grey under parts, yellowish green (17-18 cm.)

The Yellow-billed Grosbeak, also known as the "Chinese Grosbeak" is a handsome and familiar bird of parks and woodlands in Eastern China. Identification of this species is quite easy. Its huge yellow bill with a blackish tip, from which it derives its name is absolutely diagnostic. Another species, the Japanese Grosbeak, has a similar appearance and the large yellow bill, but it lacks the black tip.

The Yellow-billed Grosbeak is a songbird and a member of the finch family. Grosbeaks are generally bigger than other finches, and the name "grosbeak, means "large bill/beak". The enormous beak of the bird is an adaptation for feeding on the bird's favorite food, nuts. The large, thick and powerful bill is ideally suited to cracking open very hard nuts that other nut-eating birds cannot manage. This special adaptation gives this species and other grosbeaks an absolute monopoly on certain foods.

The Yellow-billed Grosbeak is considered a "locally common" species meaning that in certain parts of its range it is quite common while in other parts of its range it may be uncommon or even rare. Certainly, in Qingdao, and surrounding Shandong province this species is extremely common. It can be said for certain, however, that the species is doing well and maintaining a healthy population.

Yellow-billed Grosbeak (Photo by Charles Lam)

Yellow-rumped Flycatcher (Ficedula zanthopygia)

(13 cm.) Yellow rump; yellow throat and underparts; black head, back, wings, and tail; conspicuous white eye-line.

The Yellow-rumped Flycatcher is one of the most beautiful birds in China. It is a brightly colored flycatcher of yellow, black and white with a distinctive patch of yellow on the base of its tail providing it with its English name. Females of the species are less brightly colored than males, but still share the yellow rump, making them readily identifiable. It is also known as the "Korean Flycatcher" and the "Tricolor Flycatcher."

As with all members of the flycatcher family, it is an insectivorous species that will perch and wait for passing insects to fly by. This species is also often seen foraging along tree branches and probing tree bark in a manner similar to a tit.

This species, like many of the flycatcher family, is highly migratory and travels far from its summer breeding grounds to spend winter. In summer, this bird breeds in East Asia including West Japan, Korea, and much of northeast China as far south as Shandong Province. Following its fall migration, this species can be found in a wide range of South Asia as far west as parts of India. It shows a fondness for all types of forest for nest-building and breeding.

All flycatchers make very neat, cup-shaped nests that are often lined with materials such as hair and decorated with moss.

All flycatchers sit on their perches with a distinctive posture. They sit upright with their bodies at close to a 90 degree angle to their perch. Other bird species perch with their bodies in a less upright position.

Thankfully, the beautiful Yellow-rumped Warbler is a common and successful species that can be often found with little effort. During its spring and fall migrations, it is can be found in city parks, especially beside small rivers and streams.

Yellow-rumped Flycatcher <u>Devonpike</u> at <u>English Wikipedia</u>

Zitting Cisticola (Cisticola juncidis) Zong shanweiying
(10 cm.) Small; heavily streaked back; white tip on tail; reddish-brown rump

The Zitting Cisticola is a small bird which used to be included in the family of warblers. This species, along with other cisticolas and prinias, now constitute the family, "Cisticolidae." Its former name is "Streaked Fantail Warbler."

The Zitting Cisticola looks like a small brown warbler with its slender body and long, thin bill. Its bill is an adaptation for capturing the insects which form the large part of its diet. As its former name suggests, this species is heavily streaked with black on its brown back. Its white-tipped tail is often spread widely open like a fan. The underparts of this bird are white.

This species is found in grasslands near water where large numbers of insects are likely to be found. Cisticolas are generally non-migratory birds that live in warm climates that can offer an insect population all year long. It is a resident bird throughout its Chinese range as it is only found in the southeast of the country from just south of Shanghai in the north down to the South Coast including Hainan and Taiwan.

The nesting season of the Zitting Cisticola is generally in accordance with the rainy season during its breeding season. The male of the species builds the foundation of a nest, and he display the quality of his craftsmanship to prospective mates as part of his courtship efforts. If a female accepts his invitation to mate, the pair of birds will complete the nest together. The male bird will also hover above a prospective female while calling to her during courtship.

The female lays 3-6 eggs in the completed nest which is a cup shaped structure with a canopy for protection. The Zitting Cisticola is a polygamous species which will change mates and raise more than one brood per breeding season.

Zitting Cisticola (Photo by JM Garg)

###